Hat-Tricks

A virologist by profession, Kersi Meher-Homji is 'a notable
addition to the ranks of Australian cricket writers', according
to Ray Robinson.

Hat-Tricks is Kersi's sixth cricket book following *Cricket's
Great Families*, 1980 (reprinted in 1981), *1000 Tests*, 1984,
Parsee Cricket Centenary, 1986, *Out for a Duck*, 1993
(reprinted in 1994) and *The Nervous Nineties*, 1994.

He has also contributed to *The Oxford Companion of
Australian Sports* (1992, 1994) and to *The Oxford Companion
of Australian Cricket* (to be released in 1996). He freelances
for the *Sydney Morning Herald, Australian Cricket, Wisden
Cricket Monthly* (England) and is the sports editor of the
Indian Down Under.

The author comes from a cricketing family including an
uncle who played in a Test and a grand uncle who topped
1000 runs when an official All India team toured England in
1911.

'I have known Kersi for many years and respect him as a
cricket journalist and author of distinction,' writes Michael
Whitney in the Foreword.

To quote David McNicoll from *The Bulletin*, Kersi 'is the
first person I have encountered who can make a cricket book
interesting for a non-cricket fan. Quite an achievement.'

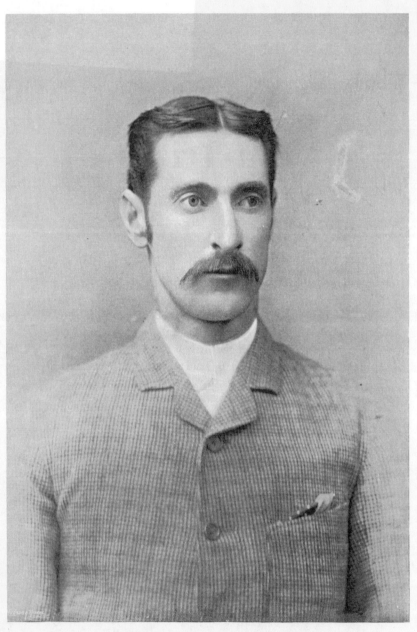
'Demon' Spofforth, the pioneer of hat-tricks.

HAT-TRICKS

Kersi Meher-Homji

Kangaroo Press

Dedicated to the memory of

Bapoo B. Mama

A true friend and an inspiration

Cover design by **Darian Causby**

Cover Photo: A spectacular diving catch by David Boon at short leg and Shane Warne completes his hat-trick in the Melbourne Test, 29 December 1994. *(Patrick Eagar)*

First published in 1995 by Kangaroo Press Pty Ltd
3 Whitehall Road Kenthurst NSW 2156 Australia
P.O. Box 6125 Dural Delivery Centre NSW 2158
Printed by Griffin Paperbacks, Netley, South Australia

ISBN 0 86417 736 4

Contents

Postscript

English all-rounder Dominic Cork took a hat-trick in the Manchester Test against the West Indies in the opening over of the fourth and final day, 30 July 1995. His victims were quality batsmen, captain Richie Richardson (bowled for 22), Junior Murray (lbw 0) and Carl Hooper (lbw 0). In quality of batsmen dismissed, it can be ranked in the Top 4 category; after Jack Hearne's in 1899, Damien Fleming's in 1994-95 and Peter Petherick's in 1976-77.

By a remarkable coincidence, Cork's only other first-class hat-trick, for Derbyshire v. Kent at Derby in 1994, was also completed by trapping Hooper lbw for nought. His other victims were Kent skipper and opening batsman M. R. Benson (bowled for 24) and no. 3 bat M. J. Walker (lbw 0).

Of the 20 bowlers to perform 22 hat-tricks in 119 years of Test cricket, Cork made the highest score, an unbeaten 56. The only other Test hat-tricker to score a fifty in the same match was Englishman Billy Bates (55 runs) in the Melbourne Test of 1882-83.

From October 1994 to July 1995 has been a prolific period for Test hat-tricks; three in 10 months (Fleming's in Rawalpindi on 9 October 1994, Shane Warne's in Melbourne on 29 December 1994 and, more recently, Cork's).

Foreword

'A hat-trick is without peer the bowlers' holy grail', says Michael Whitney.

The phrase 'he's taken a hat-trick!' is one of astonishment to cricket's loyal followers. It is without peer, the bowler's 'holy grail'.

You are lucky if you take a hat-trick in your cricketing life, and when you do, you will always cherish the memory. Hat-tricks have played a strange part in my career and although I only took one I have vivid memories of a few more.

I achieved my only hat-trick on 7 November 1969. I was ten years old then, and playing for my school, Matraville Public. I can't remember who I played but I do remember that all three batsmen were bowled. I also recall that when I arrived home to deliver the big news to my mum, she turned around from the kitchen sink where she was preparing the evening meal and said, 'That's good, luv'. She had no idea what I was talking about. Let me add that by the time I retired in 1994, she knew all the rules, all the players and indeed the rarity of the hat-trick. The school mounted that ball and it still sits proudly among my other collectables. Very proudly.

When I made my debut for the 'Blues' (NSW), the hat-trick again played a big part in my life. My debut match was for NSW against Queensland at the Gabba in October 1980. My first wicket on the opening day was of Wayne Broad, whom I bowled leg stump. Great, I thought, my first victim, and a Queenslander! Ray Phillips, their wicket-keeper, was next in and a bouncer was the greeting from young Mike Whitney. It was a beauty that caught the shoulder of the bat and flew through to Steve Rixon, our keeper. Out! Two wickets in two balls.

Then in the middle as the boys were slapping me on the back, someone said 'Bowl it straight, mate, and you'll get this hat-trick'. Hat-trick! I looked around and the man coming to the wicket was Geoff Dymock, great left-arm seamer but not the world's best batsman. I went back to my mark. The thought of a 'hatty' on debut was enough—let alone my first three wickets in first-class cricket.

I ran in like the wind and bowled right on the middle stump just short of a yorker length. Dymock leaned forward and casually blocked the ball back down the wicket and I picked it up at the end of my follow-through. That was that, shallow finish, eh?—and that's exactly how I felt. Empty. Like thousands before me. So close and yet so far.

Len Pascoe took a hat-trick in a match we Blues played against South Australia in Adelaide a fortnight later. I remember that because the last man out was Ashley Mallett who backed away to the leg side and was bowled leg-stump. It was a bit embarrassing for Ashley really but I gotta say Lennie bowled really quick that day.

Now to come to some of my eerie off-field experiences. I switch on the television to watch the Australia v. West Indies Test in Brisbane in 1988-89 and see Courtney Walsh take a hat-trick. Great timing, I thought. You wouldn't believe this but a week or so later, I do the same thing only to watch Merv Hughes take a hat-trick at Perth. Weird, eh!

And then just recently, I was driving back from the Hunter Valley with a mate of mine from England who was in Australia for Christmas. I switched on the car radio only to hear Shane Warne take a hat-trick against England in Melbourne and my mate got an earful all the way home! Just the coincidence of those three hat-tricks the moment I touch the electronic button is unbelievable.

I am delighted to write a foreword for Kersi Meher-Homji's book *Hat-Tricks*. I have known Kersi for many years and respect him as a cricket journalist and author of distinction. He has a genuine love and respect for the great game of cricket and contributes to the *Sydney Morning Herald, Australian Cricket, Inside Edge, Wisden Cricket Monthly* and the *Indian Down Under*, to name a few. As far as books are concerned, this is Kersi's hat-trick, having published *Out for a Duck* in 1993 and *The Nervous Nineties* in 1994. Both were excellent reads.

Hat-Tricks includes not only well-compiled facts at Test, Sheffield Shield and junior levels but also dramatic moments, curiosities and humour. The final chapter on 'Tall Tales and True' includes never-before-published stories and experiences of club cricketers, some of which could only be described as Ripleyesque.

The hat-trick will always be a special achievement for any bowler, as very few have been taken at the highest level. Almost all are remembered with passion. My only other 'hat-trick' occurred in June 1994, when our triplets Fergus, Madeliene and Juliette were born.

Michael Whitney
June 1995

Acknowledgments

*It is not so much our friends' help that helps us
as the confident knowledge that they will help us.*
— Epicurus

The numero uno on my list to thank is Michael Whitney, the Mr
Popular who found time to pen the inspiring Foreword in between
playing Masters Cup Cricket in Bombay, TV appearances in
Gladiators, Hard Yards and *Sydney Weekender*, his varied
promotional and business transactions and, I suspect, baby-sitting
for his triplets.

Seeded no. 2 on my thankyou list is editor Carl Harrison-Ford, no
relation to the Hollywood actor. It was Carl who suggested, after a
few drinks at the Cricketers' Club in Sydney, 'Why don't you write
a book on hat-tricks?'

I thank Lindsay Kline and Damien Fleming for sharing with me—
and readers of this book—their hat-trick stories. My sincere thanks
to Ross Dundas for checking some of my statistics.

Many others rallied round to feed a hat-trick hungry writer:
Norman and Edna Halpin, Robert Lord, Stephen Gibbs (who dug out
references for me), Bapoo Mama—alas, no more, Erica Sainsbury,
John Chapman (librarian, NSW Cricket Association Library),
Jonathan Crisp, Ian Jessup, Dr Vasant Naik, Cliff Winning, Arthur
Watson, George Richards, Graham Clayton, Jack Brown, Tom Allom,
John Defina, Andrew Samson and George Turnbull.

My special thanks to Tricia Ritchings for her word-processing
expertise, and everyone at Kangaroo Press—especially David and
Priscilla Rosenberg and Lachlan McLaine.

I also thank Peter Christopher (the *Sydney Morning Herald*),
Norman Tasker (*Inside Edge*, Australia), and David Frith (*Wisden*

Cricket Monthly, England) for printing my plea for hat-trick stories. The response from readers was very encouraging, well over 80 letters and phone calls. Their stories—extraordinary, weird or funny—have contributed richly to the final chapter, a potpourri of original and, in most cases, substantiated anecdotes. Those whose stories have been used are acknowledged—alongside their contributions.

For photographs I thank Jack Pollard, Andrew Foulds (the *Sydney Morning Herald*), Rick Smith, Ken Piesse, David Frith, Patrick Eagar, Ronald Cardwell, Australian Picture Library, Sydney (Allsport), Marylebone Cricket Club (MCC), Michael Whitney, Rusi Surti, Steve Davies, Brian Mundin and Jonty Winch.

And thank you, Tony Rafty, for the caricature drawn especially for the book.

Feature articles by the following provided rich research material: G. B. Buckley (*The Cricket Quarterly*, Vol. 8, No. 1, Spring 1970); Major C. H. B. Pridham (*The Cricketer*, England, Vol. 13, 28 May 1932); the editor, *(The Australian Cricket*, Vol. 1, No. 2, 21 November 1947); Edward Liddle (*Wisden Cricket Monthly*, April 1984); and Robert Brooke (*The Cricketer*, England, December 1994).

Other publications regularly dipped into were several editions of *Wisden Cricketers' Almanack*, *Cricketer* (Australia), *Australian Cricket, Inside Edge, Wisden Cricket Monthly, The Cricket Statistician* (England), *The Cricketer* (England), *The Times of India, The Cricketer* (Pakistan) and *Hill Chatter*, a publication of the Sydney branch of the Australian Cricket Society.

Books consulted or quoted in brief are: *The Wisden Book of Test Cricket 1876-77 to 1977-78* by Bill Frindall (Macdonald & Jane, London, 1979); *The Wisden Book of Cricket Records* by Bill Frindall (Macdonald Queen Anne Press, London, 1986); *The Complete Who's Who of Test Cricketers* by Christopher Martin-Jenkins (Rigby, Australia, 1980); *Australian Cricket: The Game and the Players* by Jack Pollard (Hodder & Stoughton and ABC, Australia, 1982); *The Complete Illustrated History of Australian Cricket* by Jack Pollard (Pelham Books, Australia, 1992); *On Top Down Under* by Ray Robinson (Cassell Australia, 1975); *Cricket: A History of its Growth and Development Throughout the World* by Rowland Bowen (Eyre & Spottiswoode, London, 1970); *Flashman's Lady* by George Macdonald Fraser (Pan Books, London & Sydney, 1977); '*The*

Guardian Angel' (a short story, source not found); *This Curious Game of Cricket* by George Mell (Unwin Paperbacks, 1983); *Curiosities of Cricket* by Jonathan Rice (Pavilion Books Ltd, London, 1993); *Some Memorable Bowling* by Gerald Brodribb (The Cricket Book Society, England, 1946); *All Round the Wicket* by Gerald Brodribb (Sporting Handbook Ltd, London, 1951); *Cricketer Book of Cricket Disasters and Bizarre Records* edited by Christopher Martin-Jenkins (Century Publishing Co., England, 1983); *Cricket's Strangest Matches* by Andrew Ward (Robson Books, England, 1994); *Cricket Extras* and *Cricket Extras 2* by Marc Dawson (Kangaroo Press, Sydney, 1993 and 1994); *The Shell New Zealand Encyclopaedia* by Lynn McConnell and Jan Smith (Moa Beckett, 1993); *ABC Guide to Australian Test Cricketers* by Rick Smith (ABC Books, 1993); *The 'Demon' Spofforth* by Richard Cashman (NSW University Press, 1990); *Australian First-Class Cricket* by Charlie Wat (Five Mile Press, Victoria, 1993); *Making The Grade—100 Years of Grade Cricket in Sydney 1893-94 to 1993-94* by M. Bonnell, R. Cashman and J. Rogers (NSW Cricket Association, 1994); *Cricket Stories* edited by Howard Marshall (Putnam, London, 1933); *The Gillette Book of Cricket and Football* edited by Gordon Ross (Gillette Safety Razor Co, England, 1963); *England v. Australia Test Match Records 1877-1985* edited by David Frith (Willow-Collins, London, 1986); *A Century of Great New Zealand Cricketers* by Joseph Romanos (David Bateman, 1993); and *Merv Hughes* by Rod Nicholson (Magenta Press, Victoria, 1990). Every effort has been made to contact the owners of copyright.

The delightful poem *'The Church Cricketant'* by Norman Gale is taken from *The Penguin Cricketer's Companion* edited by Alan Ross (Penguin Books, England, 1979).

Introduction

Tyranny is, in fact, the uncontrolled freedom of one man.
—Dorothy L. Sayers

An author has to be careful these days. With so many cricket titles churned out every year, readers have become choosy. They demand first-hand experience, personal involvement and a certain amount of pathos. They read the blurb within and on the back cover and the pretend authors get the flick. Back goes the book to the shelf with a thud, banished from the Christmas tree for life.

And that is why I am confident of top sales of *Hat-Tricks*. A hat-trick, one of cricket's rarest and most emotion-charged spectacles when three crestfallen batsmen depart in three balls, all victims of the one bowler, produces euphoria for that bowler but gloom and despondency for the batsmen. Especially the third one—the unmourned statistic whom nobody remembers.

I was young and uncomplicated when I suffered such an ignominy and the psychological scars still show. It happened in a low division match in Bombay when two of my team-mates were dismissed off successive balls and I was the next man in.

On a hat-trick and I could barely walk. The bat kept slipping from my hand as I took guard. All I remember is the umpire raising his finger and the bowler hugging every fielder and the umpire, and kissing the ground like Mushtaq Ahmed did when Pakistan beat Australia by one wicket in the Karachi Test of October 1994. I was both shattered (for the first-ball duck) and elated (to be part of history) at the same time.

I had another personal interlude with hat-tricks but of the pure ecstatic kind. When playing for St Ives under-11 team against Proville at Killara Oval in Sydney on 29 October 1988, my son Zubin dismissed three batsmen—including a representative player Christian Zavecz—in three balls. I was the scorer in that match and was so excited that my fellow scorer offered me her Valium pill.

The following month, Australian spectators witnessed two eerie occurrences when the West Indies quickie Courtney Walsh and Australian folk hero Merv Hughes performed prolonged and agonising hat-tricks in successive Tests in Brisbane and Perth.

It was all quiet on Test hat-trick front for six years until Australian tormentors Damien Fleming on his Test debut in remote Rawalpindi and Shane Warne in sweltering Melbourne performed hat-tricks that aroused national interest on the eve of 1995.

To quote an ancient philosopher: 'Agony and ecstasy are same things; they arc but two and twenty paces apart'.

He must have meant hat-tricks.

Tony Rafty

1

The Guardian Angel

Ferrari may come and Ferrari may go,
but a hat-trick is forever.

My fascination with hat-tricks began before I got hooked on cricket. When about eight I read a story from an anthology of humorous fiction which I still remember in snatches.

Although the name of the author eludes me, the story was about a good Samaritan we will name John. Although a hopeless cricketer he was mad keen on the game and his one ambition was to take a hat-trick.

One night after he had finished his supper and written out cheques for various charities, who should appear on the scene from nowhere—his guardian angel. He introduced himself and said, 'You are a good man, benevolent and unselfish. Ask for a wish and it shall be granted.'

After jumping about three feet in the air in shock, John recovered, thought a while and replied: 'This Saturday I am playing for my club against our arch rivals. It is my dearest wish to take a hat-trick in this match which will enable us to beat them for the first time in six years.'

It was now the guardian angel's turn to be shocked. He hated cricket and did not have the foggiest idea as to what a hat-trick was.

'Sure you don't want a million pounds or a trip to Tahiti or a Ferrari to replace your battered old Ford?'

But John was adamant, saying, 'A Ferrari may come and a Ferrari may go, but a hat-trick is forever', and the guardian angel acceded reluctantly.

Now on to the Saturday afternoon match. The actual scores are erased from my memory but let's say John's club was dismissed for 210. The opponents were going strongly but would his captain give him a bowl? He pleaded gently at first, then firmly, but the skipper kept nodding his head, saying, 'Not in this important grudge-match, John. I promise you two overs next Saturday.'

With the score at 7 for 193, John turned aggressive, threatened to stop his financial support to the club and snatched the ball from a stunned captain's reluctant hands.

The batsman could not believe his luck and smashed his first three balls for 4, 6 and 6 as John desperately waited for his guardian angel to make a divine interception.

The score was now a hopeless 7 for 209, only two runs needed for the opposition to win in oodles of time. The next ball was another rank long hop and the batsman jumped out to clout a mighty six but suddenly developed violent cramps in both legs and was easily stumped. He had to be carried away; score 8 for 209.

The next delivery was a shocker. Pitched way outside the leg stump, it hit an invisible object and ricocheted backwards to break the stumps; 9 for 209.

One run to tie, two to win. But the last man in could not control his laughter at the previous freak dismissals. When facing another atrocious delivery, he fell heavily on the wickets—guffawing hysterically.

John's club won this grudge-and-giggle match by one run. But rather than being proclaimed an instant hero who had performed an incredible match-winning feat, John became a figure of derision and retired from the game, which delighted both his guardian angel and the captain.

This is not an isolated fictional account of hat-tricks. George MacDonald Fraser described a high-profile hat-trick by Harry Flashman—alias Afghanistan—in his delightful novel *Flashman's Lady*.

In a match at Lord's over 150 years ago, Gentlemen of Rugby scored 91. Kent replied strongly and were 50 without loss when the crowd started chanting: 'Bring on the Flash chap; Huzza for Afghanistan.' Soon the ladies joined in and 'gruff bass and piping soprano echoed around the ground'.

His skipper Tom Brown relented and brought in Flashman—a self-acclaimed war hero—to bowl. And within minutes he turned the match around by dismissing three of the greatest batsmen of the mid-nineteenth century—Nicolas Felix, Fuller Pilch and Alfred Mynn—much to the delight of the 'townies'.

Fired up by yells of 'Give them Afghan pepper, Flashy', he bowled the finest, fastest ball of his life. It was a sharp shooter which skidded past Nicolas Felix's toes when he had expected it around his ears. Before he could smother it, his stump went cartwheeling.

'The yell that went up split the heaven,' Flashman exclaimed. 'I'd not have swapped that wicket for a peerage.'

The next man in was Fuller Pilch, the best professional of his day and Flashman's boyhood hero. He was surprised by the speed and bounce of the ball, played forward but the ball popped in the air. 'Flash' dived—all arms and legs—and grabbed a freak catch. Pilch departed slapping his bat in vexation and the crowd went wild.

Felix and Pilch in two balls—what more can a man want?

The next man in was Alfred Mynn, the Lion of Kent, looking like Alfred the Great. Six feet tall, weighing nineteen stone, 'with a face like fried ham garnished with a double whisker, but now looking like Goliath', he walked in stately and magnificent, with his broad crimson sash and the bat like a kid's paddle in his hands.

Flash's third ball was dead on length but a foot outside the leg stump. Mynn let it go by and it flicked his calf and Flash sprang high in the air—completely blocking the umpire's line of vision—and appealed screamingly. Although the umpire was in no position to give a decision, he wanted to be part of history and cried out: 'Out! Yes, absolutely out. Out!'

It was bedlam after that and the 'townies' went berserk. His team-mates seized him and rolled him on the ground. Oh well, Felix, Pilch and Mynn—England's three greatest batsmen before W. G. Grace—in three balls. Fancy that!

Mynn left the arena, shaking his head and giving the umpire a Merv Hughes glare. But being a sportsman, he stopped groaning, beamed all over his big red face and approached Flashman. He took off his hat and presented it to 'Flash' with a bow and said: 'That trick's worth a new hat any day, youngster'.

Fiction apart, a hat-trick has become folklore and an integral part of the English language. The term is used to describe any three events which take place in succession; a hat-trick of triumphs, disasters or magic moments; of hockey goals and a jockey's wins, of Wimbledon aces, Ray Martin's Logies and Liz Taylor's husbands . . . When Michael Whitney's wife Debbie had triplets in mid-1994, the media proclaimed it as 'Whit's greatest hat-trick'.

Performing a hat-trick is as much a cricketing metaphor as 'bowling a googly', 'getting stumped', 'playing with a straight bat', 'bowling a maiden over', 'batting on a sticky wicket', 'having runs on the board' and the pontificating 'it's not cricket'.

It is a human trait not to be satisfied with an achievement, however rare it be. There are more outstanding feats for a bowler to aspire to; top hat-tricks (four wickets in four balls), double hat-tricks (two hat-tricks in an innings or in a match by one bowler or six wickets in six balls), triple hat-tricks (three hat-tricks in a match or a mind-boggling nine wickets in nine balls).

In minor cricket, such astounding feats have been performed and will be detailed in subsequent chapters. Perhaps the happiest hat-trick was achieved by Mr Giles, an English farmer, in 1945. To quote Edgar Storer from *The Cricketer* magazine (England) of 19 May 1945:

'A Derbyshire farmer had in succession taken two wickets with the last two balls of an over. As the fielders were changing over, a boy ran onto the field and with a country boy's unblushing directness called out: "Hey, Mr Giles, your cow's calving".

'Unperturbed, the farmer replied: "Her'll will have to wait a bit. I've got a chance of a hat-trick." When it came his turn to bowl again, the first ball was awaited with more than usual interest. And amid a yell from the villagers, the hat-trick was accomplished, the farmer leaving in great glee to attend to his increase.'

Alfred Mynn, resembling Alfred the Great and Goliath, is fictionally linked with the origin of the word hat-trick. (Picture courtesy MCC)

2

Feather in a Tyrolean Hat

The possession of a hat of a quality superior
to the owner's status would indicate that he was
a champion at the game he played. What then
could be more appropriate for a triumphant bowler?
— G. B. Buckley

It just shows that no one can be perfect. In *The Cricketer* magazine (England) of 15 July 1939, historian G. B. Buckley wrote a treatise on the 'Origin of the Hat-Trick'. The same was reproduced in the Spring 1970 edition of *The Cricket Quarterly* (England), edited by the pedantic Rowland Bowen with the following statement preceding:

'This article appeared with several printer's errors in *The Cricketer* of 15 July 1959. The errors are now corrected.'

Oddly, Bowen himself got the year of the magazine wrong—by 20 years!

How did the term hat-trick originate? Was the capturing of three wickets in successive balls equated somehow to a three-card-trick, or was it like producing three rabbits out of a hat—the ultimate in a stage magician's tricks of the trade? If only Flashman story was not fictional!

The most reliable historical information comes through Buckley's factual and painstaking research.

The term hat-trick first appeared in *The Sportsman* (England) of 29 August 1878, when Australia's celebrated bowler Fred 'Demon' Spofforth, clean-bowled three batsmen with three consecutive balls, 'thus accomplishing the hat-trick' when playing for the Australians against 18 of Hastings and Districts at The Oval. He was also the first to claim a Test hat-trick against England four months later on the Melbourne Cricket Ground on 2 January 1879.

Although a hat-trick was first named thus in print in 1878, the earliest instance of a hat being presented for one came much earlier. In September 1858, H. H. Stephenson, the famous Surrey professional, performed the feat at Sheffield for the All England Eleven (AEE) against 22 of Hallam and Staveley, thereby 'entitling himself to a new hat which was presented to him by the Eleven.'

Stephenson's three victims were caught, bowled and caught off the last two balls of an over and the first ball of the next. It appears that 1858 was his boom year for he performed three hat-tricks that summer. The previous ones were for England against Kent at Lord's (lbw, lbw and bowled) and for England v. 18 Veterans at The Oval—all three batsmen being bowled. No mention, however, was made in these two earlier instances of his being presented a hat.

Now the mystery is why he was bestowed a hat when he bagged three wickets off successive balls for AEE and not on the previous two occasions? One supposition, according to Buckley, is that the third instance marked the origin of the custom.

A second explanation is that at Lord's and The Oval, the feats were not deemed worthy of reward. Against Kent the batsmen dismissed were tail-enders and the vanquished Veterans—although batting at nos. 3, 4 and 5—were sub-standard batsmen.

Another theory is that Stephenson was remunerated in another way for his Lord's and The Oval triumphs, 'for the practice of officially rewarding meritorious performances had been started four years before.' At Lord's, brilliant batting performances by an amateur or a professional were recognised by the presentation of—oddly enough—a new ball, and later on, by a bat. It was rarely that a bowler was rewarded. (Dennis Lillee, Ian Botham, Shane Warne et al. have turned such an anomaly around this century, haven't they?) And at The Oval, ornamental bats were presented to amateur batsmen and talent money to the professionals for scoring 50 runs or more.

The actual custom of presenting a hat for a hat-trick was first mentioned in 1858 but was by no means universal. However, a letter published in *Cricket: A Weekly Record of the Game* (England) by 'An Old Harrovian' on 23 August 1900, stated that the practice of presenting hats for a hat-trick was much older. According to what the writer had heard when he was young, the custom originated about the time Lord Frederick Beauclerk flourished, from 1791 to 1825. He added:

It became custom whenever a bowler got three wickets with three following or consecutive balls to present him with a new hat. A collection of one shilling was made from each person playing, and the result was as stated. The *hat-trick*, both in name and practice, has continued ever since, and will, I hope, so remain, in recollection of our forefathers at cricket. But it is doubtful if those engaged now will be satisfied with a hat as a valuable reward for their skill and merit. Everything, however, in these days is overdone and carried to excess. Too many matches are played by far, and the noble game thereby becomes more common, and consequently less interesting and exciting than it was when fewer contests took place some fifty years back. But money rules the day at cricket, as well as with most other things just now.

Oddly, this was penned in 1900, 77 years before the Packer 'revolution' and 95 years before the rampant bribery allegations shaking the world of cricket in 1995.

Buckley refutes the hearsay history of 'An Old Harrovian' (a *nom de plume* of famous cricket historian Arthur Haygarth) with passion:

'If this [the name 'hat-trick' and practice of hat-giving originating before 1825] were so, it is indeed strange that no mention of the practice has been found in contemporary newspapers before 1858 or of the name before 1878.

'Haygarth's memory for long past events may well have rusted as a result of his having devoted the whole of his life to the compilation of *Cricket Scores and Biographies*: for he prided himself on this being a collection of facts, and in obtaining them he relied almost entirely on the written or printed word. He was, too, past his prime when this letter appeared, being 75 years old. It seems more likely that the custom originated with the All English Eleven *after* the death in 1856 of William Clarke, their founder and autocratic secretary.'

Now two questions need to be addressed: which types of hats were presented and, well, why present a hat?

At first, a white hat was given, but Edward Rutter related in *Cricket Memories* that when representing Rugby against Old Rugbeians in 1861, his hat-trick victims presented him with a Tyrolean hat with a feather in it which he proudly wore during the rest of the match. And, of course, there were variations; in some districts it was a cap, in others a straw hat. In 1885, a miniature electroplated top hat in a satin-lined case was advertised at the price of a guinea as a suitable memento for those performing the hat-trick.

Continued Buckley: 'For a long time a really good hat had been a fairly common prize to be competed for at wrestling and single-stick, and very occasionally by pick-up sides at cricket. The possession of a hat of a quality superior to the owner's social status (if honestly acquired) would indicate that he was a champion at the particular game he played. What then could have been more appropriate for a triumphant bowler?'

What indeed, but somehow I can't picture Merv Hughes, Courtney Walsh or Shane Warne in a Tyrolean hat with a feather.

3

From Demon to Wizard

Never trouble trouble till Trumble troubles you.
— Ray Robinson

Hat-tricks at Test level are so rare, you can almost see blood in them. Only 21 hat-tricks have been performed by 19 bowlers in nearly 1300 Tests spanning 119 years. In other words, one has been achieved every 62 Tests and every 5.7 years. In the same time-frame over 2060 Test centuries have been recorded, which make hat-tricks 100-fold rarer. (See postscript on page 6).

Australians have dominated at the Test hat-trick stakes. The pioneer was Fred 'Demon' Spofforth who achieved one against England on the Melbourne Cricket Ground (MCG) on 2 January 1879 in Test no. 3. He captured 13 for 110 in this Test, his second, and Australia triumphed by 10 wickets. The last three to achieve hat-tricks are also Australians; Merv Hughes against the West Indies in Perth in 1988, Damien Fleming on his Test debut in Rawalpindi and Shane 'Wizard' Warne in Melbourne—both in late 1994.

Interestingly, all four played for Victoria although Spofforth represented NSW before moving further south and was a New South Wales man when he took the inaugural hat-trick. Also, the only two bowlers to conjure *two* hat-tricks were Victorians; Hugh Trumble against England in 1901-02 and 1903-04 (both on the MCG) and T.J. (Jimmy) Matthews against South Africa at Manchester in a Triangular series in England—one in either innings in the afternoon of 28 May 1912.

Most hat-tricks, nine, have been performed by seven Australians (Lindsay Kline, another Victorian, to complement the six already mentioned), compared to seven by Englishmen, three by West Indians and one each by a South African and a New Zealander (see Appendix).

Most hat-tricks have been witnessed in Australia, nine (five in Melbourne and one each in Sydney, Adelaide, Brisbane and Perth), followed by five in England (two each at Headingley and Old Trafford, and one at Lord's), three in Pakistan (two in Lahore, one in Rawalpindi), three in South Africa (Port Elizabeth, Johannesburg and Cape Town) and one in New Zealand (Christchurch).

Three players claimed hat-tricks in their Test debuts; England's Maurice Allom who captured four wickets in five balls against New Zealand at Christchurch in 1929 -30, New Zealand off-spinner Peter Petherick against Pakistan at Lahore in 1976-77 and Fleming, also against Pakistan in Rawalpindi in 1994-95. Fleming was an excited fielder and a 'consultant' to Warne when the latter took a hat-trick in Melbourne two months later. Also, Fleming is the only player to be involved in *two* hat-tricks in his first two Tests.

Two bowlers achieved hat-tricks in their final Tests; Trumble in 1903-04 and South Africa's Geoff Griffin at Lord's in 1960, both against England. The aftertaste of hat-trick was bitter for 21-year-old Griffin because he was no-balled 11 times for throwing by umpire Frank Lee and was forced out of Test cricket. At 21 years and 12 days he was the youngest Test hat-tricker just as England's off-spinner, Tom Goddard, was the oldest to achieve this feat, aged 38 years 87 days, against South Africa at Johannesburg in 1938-39.

The first member of the 'Exclusive Hat-Trick Club' to pass away was English medium-pace all-rounder Billy Bates. Only the second bowler to perform the hat-trick (v. Australia on the MCG in 1882-83) he died in 1899. And the oldest to survive was Allom, who died in April 1995, aged 89. As mentioned before, he was the only one to take four Test scalps in five deliveries. It may be added that Eddie Barlow, the ebullient South African all-rounder, also took four wickets in five balls for Rest of the World v. England at Headingley in 1970, but the high calibre-match is not given Test status.

The only hat-tricker to score a Test century is English all-rounder Johnny Briggs. An aggressive right-hand bat, he scored 121 against Australia on the MCG in 1884-85 and seven years later took a hat-trick—the only one in Sydney—as a left-arm slow bowler.

The sole hat-tricker to turn a politician after retirement was Wes Hall, the Windies super-quickie and later a senator. No hat-tricker has been knighted.

Five bowlers achieved 'run-less' hat-tricks; all three victims shot down for ducks. They are George Lohmann (v. South Africa, Port Elizabeth, 1895-96), Jack Hearne (v. Australia, Headingley, 1899), Allom, Kline (v. South Africa, Cape Town, 1957-58) and Warne, recently in Melbourne.

And the most 'expensive' one was by Fleming in October 1994. His victims, Aamer Malik (65 runs), Inzamam-ul-Haq (0) and—after drinks break—Salim Malik (237) totalled 302 runs between them. For those keen on trivial pursuit, Fleming's hat-trick was the third interrupted by a drinks break—after Spofforth's in 1878-79 and Bates' in 1882-83.

The two most prolonged hat-tricks were performed by the West Indies fast bowler Courtney Walsh (v. Australia) and by Australian quickie Merv Hughes (v. West Indies) in consecutive Tests in Brisbane and Perth in 1988. Walsh took an incredible 45 hours to complete his hat-trick, which spanned two innings. In the very next Test, a fortnight later, Hughes achieved a weird hat-trick which spread across three overs, two innings and two days.

Although no player has performed a hat-trick when captaining his country, Trumble and Walsh led Australia (in 1901-02) and West Indies (in 1994-95), respectively.

In sheer quality, the classiest hat-trick was achieved by England's 'Old Jack' Hearne against Australia at Headingley in 1899 when he dismissed high-calibre batsmen Clem Hill, Syd Gregory and Monty Noble off successive balls for a combined total of 0.

There is a fascinating ebb and flow phenomenon in the chronology of hat-tricks. From 1878 to 1912—the pre World War I years—nine hat-tricks were performed, that is one every four years and every thirteen Tests. From 1912 to 1956 was a lean period which saw only two hat-tricks, at the rate of one every 22 years and every 161 Tests. From 1957 to 1961 as many as five were achieved; practically a hat-trick every season and every twelve Tests. Then a drought of one trick between 1961 to 1987, followed by 'floods' in 1988 and 1994—as detailed later.

Now to blow-by-blow accounts of all 21 Test hat-tricks.

'Demon' Spofforth started it in Melbourne in 1879 when in his second Test he bowled Vernon Royle (3 runs) and Francis MacKinnon

(0), and had Tom Emmett caught by Tommy Horan for 0. Spofforth was a little lucky to secure Emmett's wicket because it was a loose delivery and a little to the leg. Tall, lean and athletic, Spofforth could run 100 yards in under 11 seconds. A cricketing legend, he could mix speed, swing and cut with devilish accuracy; his basic pace was fast-medium.

His hat-trick was achieved in the first innings when he took 6 for 48 and he went on to become the first bowler to grab 10 wickets in a Test. His cleverly varied pace made him the game's first great Test bowler. He later settled in England and played for Derbyshire.

Test cricket's second hat-trick was also witnessed in Melbourne, on 20 January 1883. Medium-paced English all-rounder Billy Bates from Nottinghamshire used a spot exploited earlier by the great Aussie all-rounder George Giffen, and bowled Percy McDonnell for 3, accepted an easy return catch from Giffen (0) and had the mighty George Bonnor (0) caught by Walter Read at silly mid-on and England won the Test by an innings and 27 runs—the first victory by an innings margin in Test history.

Bates took 14 for 102 in this Test but there were controversies; 'the pitch being affected by the plates on English all-rounder Dick Barlow's boots which provided him an unfair advantage', according to some Australians. 'Prior to this game, Bates had not been a particularly damaging bowler,' wrote historian Richard Cashman in *The 'Demon' Spofforth*. The Englishmen retaliated by accusing Spofforth of 'unlawfully putting spikes in his boots to cut-up the turf.'

Bates' career came to an abrupt end when he received a blow in the eye at net-practice on the MCG, permanently damaging his eyesight—four years after his hat-trick. Always elegantly dressed, Bates was a fine singer and his rendition of 'The Bonny Yorkshire Lass' fascinated the King of the Sandwich Islands so much that he requested Bates to sing it repeatedly on the voyage to Australia.

The only bowler to take a hat-trick in a Sydney Test was Johnny Briggs, the Lancashire slow left-arm bowler. On a sodden pitch on 2 February 1892, he ended Australia's second innings by bowling Walter Giffen for 3, having Sydney Callaway caught by W. G. Grace and trapping Jack Blackham lbw for ducks in three consecutive balls. All rather pointless and frustrating to Briggs as England lost by 72 runs.

Briggs was one of the best loved Lancashire characters. A cheerful, simple man, he loved cricket and life but his end was tragic. During the Headingley Test against Australia in 1899, he suffered an epileptic seizure which ended his Test career. He died in a mental asylum.

Now to the St. Valentine's Day hat-trick which brought South African batsmen no whiff on romance. For England against South Africa at Port Elizabeth in 1895-96, all-rounder George Lohmann had mixed fortune. He made ducks in both innings but compensated by capturing 15 for 45. His second innings figures were truly marvellous: 9.4 overs, 5 maidens, 7 runs, 8 wickets—including the hat-trick which routed the opponents for 30—and England won by 288 runs.

His victims were Frederick Cook, James Middleton (both bowled) and Joseph Willoughby (caught by Tom Hayward)—all three for ducks. A tuberculosis sufferer, Lohmann settled in South Africa in 1895, managed the Springboks' tour to England in 1901 and died in his adopted country later that year.

It was left to Jack Hearne, a member of the famous cricketing family, to perform the first Test hat-trick in England. On 30 June 1899, in the second innings, he bowled Clem Hill, had Syd Gregory caught by Archie MacLaren and Monty Noble by K. S. Ranjitsinhji—the no. 3, 4 and 5 batsmen—for ducks at Headingley. It remains the most distinguished hat-trick of all time judging by the quality of batsmanship (not counting of course Harry Flashman's *fictional* hat-trick—his victims Felix, Pilch and Mynn, as detailed in Chapter 1).

Hearne took 3061 wickets in first-class cricket, the fourth highest after Wilfred Rhodes (4187 wickets), A. P. 'Tich' Freeman (3776) and Charlie Parker (3278)—all being Englishmen. Also, Hearne performed four hat-tricks in first-class cricket.

Hugh Trumble, Australia's medium-pacer and occasional off-spinner, performed the next two hat-tricks. His first was on the MCG on 4 January 1902, when he completed Australia's victory with a hat-trick, dismissing Arthur Jones (caught by Joe Darling for 6), John Gunn (caught by Ernie Jones for 2) and Sydney F. Barnes (caught and bowled for nought).

Then on 8 March 1904, in his final Test on the MCG, he accomplished another hat-trick. His victims: B. J. T. Bosanquet caught by Alby Gehrs for 4, skipper 'Plum' Warner caught and bowled for 11 and 'Dick' Lilley for no score. How satisfying to end one's Test career—capturing the last seven wickets and Australia winning by

'Never trouble trouble till Trumble troubles you.' Hugh Trumble remains the only bowler to take hat-tricks in two Tests. (Jack Pollard Collection)

218 runs! He remains the only one to take hat-tricks in different Tests and the only hat-tricker to have a Test-playing brother, John.

Trumble got married between his two hat-tricks, timing the wedding to make a honeymoon trip during the Australians' 1902 tour of England. Tallest amongst the Australian skippers, he cut a conspicuous figure, telling amusing yarns after his retirement. 'His sombrero-like grey felt hat stood out like a mushroom among toadstools,' wrote Ray Robinson in *On Top Down Under*. 'These hats with the widest brims west of Mexico, he imported from the United States'.

'Never trouble trouble till Trumble troubles you,' wisecracked Robinson, Australia's best and wittiest cricket author.

After a lapse of eight years, Australian leg-spinner Jimmy

Matthews performed Test cricket's *only* double hat-trick. On a cloudy Old Trafford afternoon on Saturday, 28 May 1912, he achieved cricket immortality in six balls; achieving two hat-tricks in a session.

And to think that truly great bowlers like Charles 'Terror' Turner, S. F. Barnes, Bill O'Reilly, Clarrie Grimmett, Harold Larwood, Ray Lindwall, Vinoo Mankad, Alec Bedser, Jim Laker, Richie Benaud, Fred Trueman, Dennis Lillee, Hugh Tayfield, Imran Khan, Michael Holding, Richard Hadlee, Bishan Bedi, Curtly Ambrose, Kapil Dev, Craig McDermott . . . never managed one Test hat-trick between them while an unremarkable leggie like Matthews—with only 16 wickets in eight Tests—takes two in a few hours! One of the game's biggest paradoxes.

Matthews' double hat-trick was performed in Old Trafford, Manchester, against South Africa. The Test was the first of an innovative—but never since repeated—Triangular tournament between England, Australia and South Africa. All nine Tests were played in England. Australia was not at full strength, and the South Africans provided weak opposition. Back to the Matthews Test. On the first day of what became a two-day Test, Australia scored 448 and the opponents were 1-16 at stumps.

The second day started promisingly for them with Aubrey Faulkner (112 not out), Gordon White and Rolland Beaumont going well and the score on 7 for 265 at 4 p.m. when Matthews struck. Pint-sized but 'as tough as a piece of jarrah', he clipped Beaumont's off bail for 31 and trapped Sid Pegler and Tommy Ward lbw for ducks. They collapsed from 7 for 265 to 265 all out, Faulkner stranded partnerless.

Forced to follow-on, Faulkner went in first but was out for a duck and the beleaguered Springboks were soon 5 for 70. Matthews was at it again bowling Herbie Taylor for 21. Reggie Schwarz faced Matthews' next ball, a slower delivery which he cocked up in the air. The bowler dived to the right and caught it one-handed. That brought in wicket-keeper Ward—uniquely facing a Matthews hat-trick again—perhaps mumbling 'Why me? Tell me that this is a nightmare!'

To quote Andrew Ward (no relation, apparently) in *Cricket's Strangest Matches*: 'With fielders all around, hovering for the kill, he [Ward] popped the ball into the air. There was a lull while fielders decided on responsibility. Matthews himself took the initiative, diving full length, holding the ball close to the ground, then throwing it in the

Pint-sized but tough as a piece of jarrah, T. J. Matthews took two hat-tricks in one session in the Manchester Test of 1912. Photo: *(Jack Pollard Collection)*, Illustration (David Frith and *Wisden Cricket Monthly*)

air with the delight of a man who has snared the same hat-trick victim twice in a match. Curiously, these six wickets were the only ones Matthews took in the match and none needed help from a fielder.'

After 17 hat-trick-free years, the tall English fast medium swing bowler Maurice Allom broke the drought. In New Zealand's historic first ever Test, he became the first bowler to perform a hat-trick in his Test debut and remains the only English amateur to achieve it. On a fast Christchurch pitch on 10 January 1930, New Zealand were sent in to bat. They were already struggling at 3 for 21 when Allom sent back four batsmen in five balls in his eighth over; the last three off successive deliveries. Swerving the ball sharply in buffeting wind, he started with bowling 'Stewie' Dempster for 11 and after a dot ball sent back Tom Lowry (lbw), Ken James (caught behind by 'Tich'

Cornford) and Ted Badcock (bowled) for triple debut ducks and the Kiwis were gasping for oxygen at 7 for 21.

After retirement Allom, in collaboration with Test and Cambridge University colleague Maurice Turnbull, wrote humorous accounts of his two major tours titled *The Book of Two Maurices* and *The Two Maurices Again*. Later he served as President of MCC (1969-70) and President of Surrey (1971-79).

A versatile personality, he played tenor and baritone saxophone in Fred Elizalde's jazz band at The Savoy in 1927, three years before his sensational Test bow.

Boxing Day, 1938, saw English off-spinner Tom Goddard perform a hat-trick in the Johannesburg Test. He caught and bowled Dudley Nourse for 73, had Norman Gordon stumped by Les Ames and bowled W. W. 'Billy' Wade for ducks. Originally, Goddard was a mediocre fast-medium bowler for Gloucestershire but at 29 started bowling off-spin with dramatic effect. Tall (190 cm) and with enormous hands, he could turn the ball sharply and was a master of flight. Colleagues and opponents recall his appeal, a rolling, burring 'How we're it?'

Nineteen years elapsed before the next hat-trick. The hero of the first post-WWII hat-trick was Englishman Peter Loader, the Surrey paceman who later became a Test commentator and is settled in Western Australia. A hostile, wiry fast bowler with a long, high-stepping run-up, Loader spearheaded Surrey's attack with Alec Bedser during their triumphant Championship years of 1952 to 1958. His bouncer, however, was sometimes considered suspect.

On a cold, overcast day, 25 July 1957, at Headingley, the West Indies lost four wickets in four balls—collapsing from 6 for 142 to 142 all out. Fred Trueman started the rot bowling 'Collie' Smith off the last ball of his 17th over. Then Loader, who had already taken 3 for 36 in 20 overs, started his vanishing trick, yorking skipper John Goddard for 1, had 'Sonny' Ramadhin caught by Trueman for 0 and bowled Roy Gilchrist for another duck.

Lindsay Kline, a left-arm acrobatic off-break and googly bowler, performed a hat-trick on 3 January 1958, against South Africa in Cape Town. He ended the match soon after lunch on the fourth day dismissing Eddie Fuller (caught by Richie Benaud), Hugh Tayfield (lbw) and Neil Adcock (caught by Bob Simpson) for noughts and Australia won by an innings.

The Windies celebrating Lance Gibbs' hat-trick in the Adelaide Test of 1961; the first in Australia in 57 years. (*Adelaide Advertiser*)

Kline's other magic moment was in the Adelaide Test against the West Indies in 1961. A poor batsman, he hung on for 100 minutes adding 65 match-saving runs with Ken Mackay to force a draw.

The exciting Adelaide Test of 1961 is also remembered for Lance Gibbs' hat-trick on 30 January, when in the first innings the Windies offie trapped Ken Mackay lbw for 29, Wally Grout caught by Garfield Sobers for 0 and Frank Misson bowled for 0 in three balls. In the previous Test in Sydney, Gibbs had dismissed Mackay, Johnny Martin and Grout in four deliveries.

A lithe, pencil-thin off-spinner with long fingers, Gibbs is the only spinner to capture more than 300 Test wickets and was a record-holder for a few years. With an unorthodox chest-on action and clever synchronisation of his arms, he exploited every conceivable change of pace, flight and length. A cousin of Test captain Clive Lloyd, Gibbs was an expert at forecasting horseracing results.

Two hat-tricks were sandwiched between Kline's in 1958 and Gibbs' in 1961. Wes Hall achieved one in Lahore on 29 March 1959, and there was a controversial one by Geoff Griffin at Lord's on 23 January 1960.

Consistently fast, hostile and graceful, Hall became the first from the West Indies to take a hat-trick. He trapped Mushtaq Mohammad—the youngest Test debutant at 15 years and 125 days—lbw for 14, had Fazal Mahmood caught by Sobers for 0 and then bowled Nasim-ul-Ghani for another duck.

A muscular 188-cm man with a classical action, Hall was a fearsome prospect—especially in partnership with Roy Gilchrist and Charlie Griffith. He possessed a long, smooth run-up, with eyes bulging, gold teeth glinting and a crucifix swinging across his chest. He was a joy for spectators but a Nemesis for the batsmen.

Eight months after Hall, the blond South African rookie Geoff Griffin, 21, had an ecstatic-traumatic experience in the Lord's Test in January 1960. After the ecstasy of becoming the first South African to perform a Test hat-trick and the first—and the only one so far—to do it at Lord's, he plunged into the depression of a rejected hero.

In only his second Test—and as it turned out, his last—Griffin had Mike J. K. Smith caught by John Waite for 99 with the last ball of an over and then bowled Peter Walker for 52 and Trueman for nought off the first two balls of his next over.

Unfortunately, he was called 11 times by umpire Frank Lee for throwing. His humiliation continued in an exhibition match played after the Test when umpire Sid Buller persistently no-balled him and he had to finish his last over underarm. Griffin's 'throw' action was attributed to an injury at school which left him with a distinct crook of

Wes Hall's rhythmic run-up. He is the first West Indian to take a Test hat-trick.
(Sydney Morning Herald)

the right elbow and he was totally unable to straighten the arm naturally.

After a 15-year lull on the hat-trick front, New Zealand off-spinner Peter Petherick performed a dramatic Test debut hat-trick against Pakistan in Lahore on 10 October 1976. It was a fairytale stuff for 'Pizzle' Peter, an easygoing, laconic motor mechanic from Alexandria. He was delighted to play his initial first-class match aged 33 and Test cricket was then furthest from his mind. But after taking 9 for 93 against Northern Districts (which included Test star John Wright) in the first innings, he was picked on the tour of Pakistan and India in 1976.

The Kiwi bowlers were plundered by Paki greats Javed Miandad and Asif Iqbal who put on 281 glorious runs in under four hours when new boy Petherick struck in his 16th over. First he had Test debutant Miandad caught by Richard Hadlee for 163, then took a comfortable, if low, caught and bowled to remove Wasim Raja first ball. Intikhab Alam came in next and Geoff Howarth at silly point dived forward to take an acrobatic catch. Sportingly, 'Inti' walked after the umpire showed no interest in giving him out. In quality of batsmen, this was perhaps the second best hat-trick after Jack Hearne's and the best this century.

Laid-back Peter commented in a deadpan voice: 'I always knew I'd do it. I just gave them 97 runs to loosen up!'

He played only five more Tests and disappeared from the scene as quickly and quietly as he had entered. Like Jimmy Matthews of the double hat-trick fame, he took only 16 Test wickets. But for these hat-tricks, Matthews and Petherick would have been forgotten today.

After 11 years and 318 Tests of hat-trick abstinence which coincided with major changes in cricket—the Packer 'revolution', limited-overs internationals, coloured clothing, white balls—two unusual hat-tricks were performed in two Tests in November-December 1988.

Surprisingly, neither Courtney Walsh nor his team-mates nor opponents knew that a hat-trick was performed by him in the Brisbane Test till a few balls later. It was the most prolonged hat-trick in Test history and took 45 and a half hours to complete. It started with Tony Dodemaide being caught by Vivian Richards off Walsh for 22. It was Richards' 100th catch in his 100th Test and Australia were all out for 167 on 18 November 1988.

West Indies replied with 394, a big lead of 227. At 2 for 65 in Australia's second innings on 20 November, Walsh came on to bowl. Mike Veletta pulled his first ball to mid-on and was caught by Carl Hooper for 10. His second ball found Graeme Wood—Valetta's brother-in-law—palpably leg before for a duck. Next man in was skipper Allan Border, nursing a broken finger, and determined not to get out first ball to avoid a hat-trick. Belatedly it dawned on the players—aided by a public announcement—that Walsh had already achieved the feat—his three victims in three balls being Dodemaide (two days before), Valetta and Wood.

Curiously, Merv Hughes (whose motto in life must be: 'Anything you can do, I can do it whackier') achieved a weird hat-trick in the very next Test in Perth. The stout-hearted, heavily moustachioed, never-say-never fast bowler Hughes took 13 wickets in the Test (including 8-87 in the second knock) and yet Australia lost by 169 runs.

Hughes ended the Windies first innings by having Curtly Ambrose caught by Ian Healy with the last ball of his 36th over and Patrick Patterson caught by Dodemaide with the first ball of his next which ended the visitors' innings at 449 on 3 December. Border declared Australia's innings closed at 8 for 395 after fast bowler Geoff Lawson, wearing a visorless helmet, lost sight of a lifting ball from Ambrose which shattered his jaw.

The sight of Lawson's fractured jaw infuriated Hughes. His first ball of the innings trapped the Windies' opening batsman Gordon Greenidge leg before which gave the moustachioed Merv a unique hat-trick spanning two days, two innings and three overs.

Hughes was probably inspired by Bob Hawke, the then Prime Minister of Australia. Persuaded to give a ball-by-ball commentary on ABC radio, the cricket-loving PM 'took' a wicket with his first ball on the microphone. He continued till the end of West Indies first innings which included the first two wickets in Hughes' interrupted hat-trick.

The hat-tricks by Damien Fleming in October 1994, and by 'Wizard' Warne two months later are fresh in our mind. They are related in 3-D effect by the bowlers themselves in the next chapter.

One of the inspiring nevers of Test cricket is the feat of taking four wickets in four balls. It remains as elusive as an individual Test score of 400 runs.

4

In Their Own Words

Salim doesn't know it yet, but he's about to become a part of Test history.
— **Damien Fleming**

In this chapter, cricketers give their stories (actual happenings and emotional background) of taking a Test hat-trick.

MAURICE ALLOM
(First Test, England v. New Zealand, Christchurch, 10 January 1930)

Maurice passed away in April 1995, aged 89, soon after receiving my request for the story on his unique hat-trick (four wickets in five balls in his Test debut). His son Tom wrote this charming letter which is reproduced below:

I thank you for your letter to my father of February 19 and must apologise for taking so long to reply. I am sorry that I have to bring you the sad news that the grand old man passed away last month. I am pleased to say, however, that your letter arrived via the Oval before the event—there has been a mountain of papers to sort through and deal with, otherwise I would have found it sooner!

I know how much he enjoyed hearing from you. He was very modest about his cricketing achievements but loved it when others were interested. I am only sorry that he was unable to reply to you in person. Those were proud days for him and he kept the famous ball with a silver plaque on it inscribed with the scorer's legend of that magic over. Needless to say, that is a trophy which will be treasured for ever. I wish I could describe to you exactly how he felt on that epic day, but only he would be able to do that. I only know that it was one of the high points in the life of a charming man who was endowed with great talent, wit and kindness.

He died very peacefully, living life to the full until the very last moment at the age of 89. A great innings.

LINDSAY KLINE
(Second Test, Australia v. South Africa, Cape Town, 3 January 1958)

'We batted first, making 449. South Africa were then dismissed for 202, Richie Benaud taking 4 for 94 and myself 3 for 29. Johnny Waite was my first wicket in a Test. Alan Davidson made the initial breakthrough with two wickets when South Africa followed on. Richie Benaud then tore the heart out of the South African batting with five wickets.

I was brought back for my eleventh over. My second ball was a leg-break to which Eddie Fuller played forward and was caught by Richie at silly mid-on. The next ball, a quicker delivery, went straight on to have Hughie Taylor lbw.

As our skipper Ian Craig and I discussed the field placings for the next ball, I thought to myself that this one is for the *Hat-Trick*. The field was finally set with a number of close-in fieldsmen. I was undecided on which type of ball to bowl to Neil Adcock, the next

Left: Lindsay Kline's kangaroo leap. He took a hat-trick in his second Test.
(Jack Pollard Collection)

Above: Kline: 'I was amazed when told that the previous hat-trick by an Australian was in 1912; almost 46 years ago.'
(Rick Smith)

man, on my approach. Should I make it a googly or a chinaman (which is my leg break, as I am a left-arm bowler).

I selected a googly, which pitched off-stump, Adcock played forward, the ball caught the outside edge and carried to first slip where Bobby Simpson took a great catch. And we won!

There was then great excitement for our Test win by an innings and on my hat-trick. It took some two to three days for me to finally let it sink in that I had taken a Test hat-trick. I was amazed when told that the previous hat-trick by an Australian was in 1912.

One of the special things I remember is being given the honour of leading our team from the field, even though Richie Benaud was the star of the show.'

PETER 'PIZZLE' PETHERICK
(First Test, New Zealand v. Pakistan, Lahore, 10 October 1976)

'The only thing was, I was getting slaughtered like everyone else; my first 16 overs yielded 0 for 97. That's the thing over there [in Pakistan]. You can bowl a lot of maidens, but then you can concede a lot of 12-run overs.

Javed Miandad (163) and Asif Iqbal (166) had recovered the Pakistan innings but just before tea, Javed tried to put my delivery over the fence and got only a top edge to Richard Hadlee, standing by the square-leg umpire,' he told Joseph Romanos in *A Century of Great New Zealand Cricketers*.

Wasim Raja was next in and he came down the wicket. I was bowling round the wicket to him and he hit it straight back to me for the caught and bowled.

Intikhab Alam came in, and I never even thought about the hat-trick. The players were crowding the bat. As I went back, I thought to myself "If I was Intikhab, I would come down the wicket", and so I darted one to him. He got a glove or a hand to it and Geoff Howarth made a great catch.

Everybody appealed and as I turned around to the umpire, he was unmoved. I thought he was not going to give it but then his finger went up. However, it was only *after* Intikhab had walked that he did it.'

Laconic, genial Petherick added, tongue-in-cheek: 'I always knew I'd do it. I just gave them 97 runs to loosen up'.

A happy Healy with a beaming Hughes. *(Ken Piesse Library)*

MERV HUGHES
(Second Test, Australia v. West Indies, Perth, 3 and 4 December 1988)

Merv's great moment in his on-off Test career came in the Perth Test against the West Indies in December 1988. Before that he had played seven Tests without achieving much. Earlier, skipper Allan Border's tongue-lashing on his 'personal inflation' (meaning bulging waist line) had stirred him into action.

Despite taking 13 wickets in the Test (5 for 130 and 8 for 87) and performing a unique hat-trick, Hughes was a sad man because Australia had lost badly, according to Rod Nicholson's book *Merv Hughes*. Merv was mulling over the defeat when team manager Ian McDonald congratulated him on his winning the Man of the Match award.

'Merv broke down,' McDonald recalls. 'And it wasn't because of joy. He was so upset about Australia losing that he had forgotten his hat-trick and his bag of wickets and just did not want to know about the reward. He kept repeating "I don't want the damn thing".'

Hughes was happy and proud that his hat-trick was the only one in a Perth Test and was the first by an Australian for about 31 years— the last being by Lindsay Kline in January 1958. Of course, the last hat-trick in Test cricket was only a fortnight earlier, by the Windies quickie Courtney Walsh in the previous Brisbane Test. Ironically, Walsh was the only batsman not to fall to Hughes at Perth, remaining unbeaten in both innings.

Hughes was cut-up because his mate and partner-in-pace Geoff Lawson was struck by a bouncer from Curtly Ambrose and had to be carried off on a stretcher. Having already captured two in a row in the first innings, Hughes bowled in anger. His first ball to opener Gordon Greenidge was fast and straight and trapped him lbw. The crowd cheered lustily in revenge, although few then realised that it was a hat-trick till Steve Waugh informed Merv later.

Merv did not celebrate the hat-trick that night. Within half an hour of leaving the field he was in the minibus with other team mates on the way to see Lawson, the cricketer with the fractured jaw.

About the hat-trick, Hughes said: 'That will look good on my record. But there are more important things to worry about. There is a team-mate in hospital.'

Merv Hughes with his 'trophy'. *(Ken Piesse Library)*

Gee, what a feeling. Walsh dismisses Craig McDermott and the Windies
win the 1993 Adelaide Test by one run. *(Ken Piesse Library)*

DAMIEN FLEMING
(Second Test, Australia v. Pakistan, Rawalpindi, 9 October 1994)

'You don't think about a hat-trick in your first Test. I was just
delighted to be picked and bowl alongside "Billy" [McDermott]. To
take four wickets in the first innings was a bonus. In the second
innings, the Pakistani bats hung in for a long time and "Billy" started
bowling with a short run-up.

I also shortened my run-up by about six metres and reverted to
my Lancashire League run-up. It had immediate effect as Aamer
Malik on 65 had a whack at the ball and was caught by Michael
Bevan. With the very next ball, I bowled a yorker and trapped
Inzamam-ul-Haq lbw. It was especially pleasing because in the
previous Test in Karachi, it was his unbeaten fifty which had guided
Pakistan to a one-wicket win.

That dismissal marked the end of my over, and then came drinks.
I tried not to think about the hat-trick but could not. I told "Billy",
which proved prophetic: "Salim doesn't know it yet, but he's about
to become a part of Test history".

All of our players knew about the possibility of a hat-trick except
double centurion Salim Malik. Jo Angel bowled an over conceding

'You don't think about a hat-trick in your first Test', Fleming. *(Rick Smith)*

Damien Fleming's hat-trick in the Rawalpindi Test. He dismissed Inzamam-ul-Haq for a duck as his second victim (left). Off his next delivery he had double centurion Salim Malik caught and Jo Angel gives Damien a merry-go-round. *(Australian Picture Library / Allsport / Botterill)*

nine runs. Then came my first ball of the next over. It moved away from Salim, he edged it and became one of Ian Healy's five victims in the innings. Salim did not walk till the neutral umpire Karl Liebenberg lifted his finger.

Initially there was stunned silence, then a burst of applause for Salim, for me—I suppose, for cricket. It was one of the best balls I bowled, an outswinger. Big Jo Angel picked me up in air in jubilation, then spun me round which was a tremendous feeling. It was just amazing.'

But there is a sequel to this story as I hand over the mike back to Fleming, a friendly quickie. 'In my very next Test in Melbourne two months later, Shane Warne was on a hat-trick against England. After he had dismissed Phillip DeFreitas and Darren Gough off successive balls, he approached me and asked what I had done in Pakistan before my hat-trick. I told him that I had bowled my stock-ball, an outswinger. So Shane bowled his stock-ball, a leg-break, and got his hat-trick.

'Imagine, witnessing two hat-tricks in my first two Tests! In my next Test in Sydney, in January 1995, Darren [Gough] dismissed Mark Taylor for 49 and me the next ball for a duck to finish our first innings. Thus he was on a hat-trick when he bowled his first ball in the second innings, but it was a dot ball. Had he taken a wicket with that ball, I would have witnessed three hat-tricks in my first three Tests, a unique hat-trick of hat-tricks!'

This was Damien's fifth hat-trick of his career (including club/school cricket), and second for Australia, having taken one for the Australian Youth team at Sabina Park, Jamaica, in West Indies in 1990.

SHANE WARNE
(Second Test, Australia v. England, Melbourne, 29 December 1994)

'I was just trying to tie up an end and I got a bit lucky with three wickets,' Warne said at the press conference after his famous hat-trick on the MCG, the first by an Australian in an Ashes Test in 91 years. 'At the end I just wanted to get back into the shed and have a beer.

'I bowled a leg-spinner at Phillip DeFreitas, not trying to turn it too much. Maybe he should have come forward. It turned only a little bit. He played back and the ball kept a bit low for the lbw. I wanted next man Darren Gough to push forward. I tried for over-spin on the leggie and Ian Healy took a fine catch.'

On a hat-trick and in walked Devon Malcom, a fast bowler with no pretensions to be a batsman. He wore a helmet even for a spinner as six vulture-like fielders closed in on him. In the meantime, Warne asked Damien Fleming as to what he bowled before his Rawalpindi hat-trick. Fleming: 'I closed my eyes and bowled my stock ball, an outswinger.'

So Warne went for his stock-ball. 'I closed my eyes, pictured a leg-spinner and bowled it with some over-spin. It kicked a bit, for the bat-pad and Booney [David Boon] took a great catch.'

Umpire Steve Randell confirmed the catch with square-leg umpire Steve Buchnor before giving Malcolm out.

'It was the quickest I've ever run to get down to 'Booney'. I think I stuck my tongue in his ear,' he recalled with relish.

Shane Warne's hat-trick victim nos 1 and 2 in the 1994 Melbourne Test. He traps Phillip DeFreitas lbw (top) and next ball has Darren Gough caught by Ian Healy. *(Patrick Eagar)*

Warne's hat-trick marked the 50th Anglo-Aussie Test on the MCG and to quote David Frith from *Wisden Cricket Monthly*, 'There is no arguing with the fact that Australia played very well, with the Warne hat-trick the diamond stud.'

Warne said immediately after the match, 'I suppose I'll wake up soon.'

THE CHURCH CRICKETANT

I bowled three santicified souls
With three consecutive balls!
What do I care if Blondin trod
Over Niagara falls?
What do I care for the loon in the Pit
Or the gilded Earl in the Stalls?
I bowled three curates once
With three consecutive balls!

I caused three Protestant 'ducks'
With three consecutive balls!
Poets may rave of lily girls
Dancing in marble halls!
What do I care for a bevy of yachts
Or a dozen or so of yawls?
I bowled three curates once
With three consecutive balls!

I bowled three cricketing priests
With three consecutive balls!
What if a critic pounds a book
What if an author squalls?
What do I care if sciatica comes,
Elephantiasis calls?
I bowled three curates once
With three consecutive balls!

— **Norman Gale**
(courtesy, *The Penguin Cricketer's Companion*)

5

From the Agony End

Agony and ecstasy go together in hat-tricks,
They are only twenty-two yards apart.

Much has been written on bowlers who have achieved hat-tricks. But what about the depressed, befuddled and at times masochistic batsmen who make it possible? They come, take guard, look around for deep fine leg traps, nervously chat up the square-leg umpire and a cluster of close-in fielders and are promptly dispatched to the pavilion in successive deliveries.

None of the 19 bowlers who performed Test hat-tricks has ever been a victim from the other, the 'agony', end. This is surprising as, with few exceptions, the hat-trickers were tail-end batsmen.

Of the 62 Test-hat-trick (THT) victims, not one is from India, Sri Lanka or Zimbabwe. This is especially surprising for the Indians, as they have played almost 300 Tests. (Incidentally, no Indian, Pakistani, Sri Lankan or Zimbabwian bowler has performed a THT either.)

Twenty-eight of the 62 THT victims have been competent batsmen. Country wise, they are:

AUSTRALIA: Percy McDonnell, George Giffen, *George Bonnor**, Clem Hill, Syd Gregory, *Monty Noble*, Ken Mackay, Tony Dodemaide, Mike Veletta and *Graeme Wood*.

ENGLAND: John Gunn, 'Plum' Warner, Mike J. K. Smith, Peter Walker, Philip De Freitas and Darren Gough.

SOUTH AFRICA: Herbie Taylor, Dudley Nourse and *W. W. 'Billy' Wade*.

WEST INDIES: John Goddard and *Gordon Greenidge*.

---

* Names in italics represent batsmen who actually conceded the hat-trick, the no. 3 batsman in the sequence.

NEW ZEALAND: Tom Lowry.

PAKISTAN: Mushtaq Mohammad, Javed Miandad, Wasim Raja, Aamer Malik, Inzamam-ul-Haq and *Salim Malik*.

Salim Malik is the highest-scoring THT batsman; he made 237 runs before falling victim to Damien Fleming's drinks-interrupted hat-trick in Rawalpindi. Another Pakistani, Javed Miandad, is next with 163, followed by Englishman Mike J. K. Smith on a nervous 99. Both Miandad and Smith were victim no. 1 in the hat-trick sequence.

With the exception of Salim Malik, all no. 3 batsmen in a THT scored ducks. Interestingly, some of them were quality batsmen; viz. Bonnor, Noble, Wade, Wood and Greenidge.

Miandad has the unique distinction of making a century and being involved in a hat-trick on his Test debut. Another notable Test debutant to be involved in a hat-trick was Mushtaq Mohammad, the youngest to play Test cricket, aged 15 years and 124 days.

Fifteen batsmen have been involved in THTs on their Test debut.

ENGLAND: Vernon Royle, Francis MacKinnon (the first two victims of Fred Spofforth's historic hat-trick)

SOUTH AFRICA: Frederick Cook, James Middleton, *Joseph Willoughby* (all three dismissed for ducks in George Lohmann's St. Valentine's Day hat-trick of 1896); Rolland Beaumont, Herbie Taylor and *Tommy Ward* (twice); Norman Gordon and *'Billy' Wade*.

NEW ZEALAND: Tom Lowry, Ken James and *Ted Badcock* (all three for ducks by debutant English bowler Maurice Allom in New Zealand's first ever Test match).

PAKISTAN: Mushtaq Mohammad and Javed Miandad.

Only one batsman has experienced the agony of a THT twice. He was Tommy Ward, the South African wicket-keeper who fell victim to Australian spinner Jimmy Matthews' unique hat-trick in both innings in the Manchester Test on 28 May 1912. In this, his Test debut, Wade was dismissed both times off the first ball he received to bag a King Pair.

He recovered sufficiently to score 459 runs at an average of 13.90 (highest score 64) in 23 Tests and made 32 dismissals (19 caught and 13 stumped). But bad luck dogged this tenacious cricketer till the end. In 1936, he was electrocuted while working in a gold mine. He was 49.

6

And the One That Got Away

*Frustration: When you have ulcers
but still aren't successful.*

A hat-trick at any level is like the tip of an iceberg. For every hat-trick accomplished there were many near misses, when a bowler sent back two batsmen in two balls but the third one just would not cooperate.

It is as frustrating as scoring a ninety or missing a plane by seconds or losing your voice on the eve of an audition. Even at Test level, it would be difficult—and rather pointless—to keep statistics of bowlers taking two in two without reaching the ultimate.

However, in Test annals there have been three instances of bowlers taking four wickets in five balls, two of four in six balls and 36 of three in four balls.

Maurice Allom's four scalps in five deliveries—including a hat-trick—in his Test debut in Christchurch in 1930 has been documented in previous chapters. England's fast-medium Chris Old and Pakistan's magnificent pace bowler Wasim Akram each took four in five balls, and Ken Cranston and Fred Titmus four in six balls; but all four bowlers failed to achieve a hat-trick. This is how it happened—or rather, did not happen:

Old was thwarted by a no-ball and then by a 'killjoy' tail-ender when twice on a hat-trick in one over. In the Edgbaston (Birmingham) Test against Pakistan in 1978, Old had Wasim Raja caught behind by Bob Taylor for 17 and clean-bowled Wasim Bari for nought. The next ball was judged a no-ball. Unperturbed, he had Iqbal Qasim caught behind and Sikander Bakht caught by Graham Roope for ducks. On a hat-trick again, Old was denied this crowning glory by last man Liaqat Ali running for a single. Thus, Old's eventful over read in the scorebook as WW nb WW1. (W standing for wicket, nb for no-ball).

Wasim Akram came close to two hat-tricks in an over in the Lahore Test against West Indies on 11 December 1990. He swung the match on the final morning by capturing the last four wickets in five balls. He had Jeff Dujon caught by Moir Khan for 3 and claimed Curtly Ambrose leg-before for 0 off successive balls. Then Ian Bishop edged the next ball just wide off Imran Khan. In the next two deliveries, Akram bowled Malcolm Marshall and had Courtney Walsh lbw for ducks which ended the Windies second innings—leaving Akram stranded. The scorebook entry for this final dramatic over read: WW1WW.

In the Headingley Test against South Africa in 1947, Ken Cranston—a dentist and a fast bowler for England—took four wickets in an over. He trapped George Fullerton lbw for 13 with the first ball and had 'Tufty' Mann caught behind by Godfrey Evans for nought. After a dot ball, he bowled Lindsay Tuckett and Ian Smith off his fifth and sixth balls. This ended South Africa's second innings and also his hope for a hat-trick. His scorebook entry was W0W0WW (0 standing for no runs and no wickets, also called a dot ball).

English Test off-spinner Fred Titmus' scorebook entry for an over was an equally laudable W0WW0W against New Zealand in the Headingley Test of 1965. In a sensational spell, he dismissed Bryan Yuile for 12, Bruce Taylor, Dick Motz and Richard Collinge for noughts in his 21st over, and New Zealand collapsed from 5 for 158 to 166 all out. The Kiwis lost by an innings, minutes before rain left the ground waterlogged.

So far, 33 bowlers have taken three wickets in four balls 36 times; Fred Spofforth, Dennis Lillee and Wasim Akram achieving it twice. (For complete list, see Appendix). Coincidentally, the list is again from 'Demon' to 'Wizard', Spofforth being the first to grab 3 in 4, (Australia v. England, The Oval in 1882) and Shane Warne being the last so far to do so, v. England in the Brisbane Test of November 1994.

'Warney' had Graham Gooch caught behind by Ian Healy for 56, bowled a bemused Phillip DeFreitas behind his legs for 11 two balls later and trapped Martin McCague lbw for a first-ball duck with his flipper to get his three victims in four balls. He was on a hat-trick but missed it by a whisker, the ball just shaving Phil Tufnell's stumps. A few overs later Warne bamboozled Tufnell who 'collapsed in a heap as he tried to pad Warne away, finishing in a yoga pose which refreshingly had Australians and Englishmen all laughing together', to quote David Frith from *Wisden Cricket Monthly*.

Earlier, in 1972, Lillee took three wickets in four balls *twice* in the 1972 series, in the first Test at Old Trafford (Manchester) and in the final Test at The Oval. At Old Trafford, he dismissed Ray Illingworth (currently England's 'El Supremo'), John Snow and Norman Gifford, and at The Oval, his victims were Peter Parfitt, Illingworth and Snow. Lillee's 31 wickets in the rubber set a record for Australia in England.

Australia's Johnny Martin took a famous 3 in 4 in his Test debut, v. West Indies on the MCG in 1960-61. He sent back a trio of all-time great batsmen, Rohan Kanhai for 25, Garry Sobers (0) and Frank Worrell (0) in four balls—the last two caught by Bob Simpson. Two of his victims—Sobers and Worrell—were later knighted, which remained a matter of immense pride and joy for this popular left-arm googly bowler. He also made an uninhibited 55 in this Test, batting at no. 10. Nicknamed 'Little Fave', Johnny was everybody's favourite. Despite his small size, he gave the ball a tremendous clout and hit more than 160 sixes for his Petersham club in Sydney.

Apart from Spofforth and Warne, Lance Gibbs and Wes Hall have achieved both hat-tricks and near hat-tricks (three wickets in four balls).

The major disappointment in Fred Trueman's otherwise fabulously successful Test career was his failure to take a hat-trick despite coming near it six times. It may be added that he performed four hat-tricks in first-class cricket.

Like Johnny Martin, he came close to a hat-trick in his Test debut, the Headingley Test of 1952 remembered for India's disastrous start of losing four wickets without a run on the scoreboard in the second innings. He dismissed Madhav Mantri and Vijay Manjrekar (who had scored a century in the first innings) off successive balls but the third ball 'shaved skipper Vijay Hazare's off-stump by a lick of paint', said Trueman.

In the final Test against Australia at The Oval in 1964, Trueman approached an electrifying hat-trick. Playing his 65th Test match, he removed Ian Redpath's middle stick off the first ball of the last over before lunch. The next ball he had Graham McKenzie caught by Colin Cowdrey in the slips. He had thus captured his 298th and 299th Test victims off consecutive balls.

It appeared like something out of a soap opera. Trueman on his 300th Test wicket—a landmark never before approached—with the chance of a hat-trick! To add to the suspense, the umpire called 'lunch' at this stage.

It was an uneasy, tension-filled lunch for all—especially for 'Fiery' Fred and Neil Hawke, the next man in. Will Trueman capture his 300th Test wicket with a hat-trick? To the crowd's—and Trueman's—big disappointment, the hat-trick did not materialise. The fateful delivery passed wide of Hawke's off-stump and the sense of anticlimax was painful for all his fans.

Eventually, he had Hawke caught by Cowdrey at first slip as his historic victim no. 300, and later added Grahame Corling's scalp.

One of the saddest missed hat-tricks was by Ken Farnes, the 193-cm tall English fast bowler. In the 1938 Lord's Test against Australia, he dismissed Bill O'Reilly and Ernie McCormick off successive balls. The next man in, Chuck Fleetwood-Smith, offered a catch but Denis Compton dropped it—robbing Farnes of a hat-trick.

Three years later, Farnes was killed on active service while flying during the Second World War. He was one of the most mourned cricketers lost in the war.

Australian off-spinner Bill Howell missed out on a hat-trick in the Cape Town Test of 1902-03 when he took three wickets in four balls.

(Jack Pollard Collection)

7

Tragic Trott and Pocock Magic

Moderation is a fatal thing, Lady Hunstanton,
Nothing succeeds like excess.
— Oscar Wilde

Cricket historian Gerald Brodribb has calculated that since 1919, a hat-trick has been performed on an average six times a season in first-class matches. This adds up to a substantial number and it is beyond the scope of this book even to list them. Rather, this chapter details unusual hat-tricks in first-class cricket and concentrates on those taking four wickets in consecutive balls.

Arguably, the champion among first-class hat-trickers is Douglas Wright of Kent, who took 108 wickets in 34 Tests for England. He performed seven hat-tricks, a record he has held for almost 50 years. He is followed by Gloucestershire spinners Charlie Parker and Tom Goddard who achieved one six times each. Bowlers taking three or more hat-tricks in first-class cricket are listed in the Appendix.

The famous Hearne family had more than a nodding acquaintance with hat-tricks. Six of them took 11 hat-tricks between them in first-class cricket from 1868 to 1922 for Middlesex, Kent, MCC and/or England. Jack Hearne performed four including one in the Headingley Test of 1899. Alec and J. W. Hearne took two each and Tom, George and Walter Hearne one each.

Wisden 1995 lists 28 bowlers who have taken four wickets with consecutive balls (4 in 4) 29 times, the charismatic Bob Crisp of Western Province, South Africa, performing it twice, besides taking 4 in 5 once. He got his first 4 in 4 v. Griqualand West at Johannesburg in 1931-32, then a 4 in 5 v. Transvaal on the same venue and in the same season. In 1933-34, he again dismissed 4 in 4, v. Natal in Durban.

Crisp was an extraordinary, larger than lifesize personality. He was a fast bowler, a rugby player and a champion runner—all three at international level. But that's not all. He was a mountain climber (twice in a fortnight he conquered Mount Kilimanjaro, the second time carrying an injured friend down), soldier, journalist and author of successful war books *Brazen Chariots* and *The Gods Were Neutral*. He was tall, handsome and debonair and women found him irresistible—even at 70. Born in Calcutta, Crisp played nine Tests for South Africa, taking 20 wickets at 37.35. His best figures were 5 for 99 v. England in the Old Trafford (Manchester) Test of 1935, 'Fred' Bakewell, Wally Hammond, Bob Wyatt and Maurice Leyland being his prize scalps. But Crisp is more remembered for his top hat-tricks in 1930s. He died in March 1994, aged 82, living life to the full till the end—despite an incurable cancer and failed financial enterprises. Among the most remarkable characters who enriched the game, he believed in Oscar Wilde's maxim: 'Nothing succeeds like excess'.

The only Australian to perform 4 in 4 in Australia is Hal Hooker, for NSW v. Victoria in Sydney in 1928-29. He had figures of 28-11-

An extraordinary character, Bob Crisp is the only bowler to capture four wickets in as many balls twice.

(David Frith and *Wisden Cricket Monthly)*

42-6 (including a hat-trick) and 27-3-94-2 (which included his fourth wicket in the match off successive balls). He bowled H. I. Ebeling for 4, H. S. Gamble and Bert Ironmonger for noughts in his last over in the first innings. He continued from where he had left off, and in the second innings claimed a wicket off his first ball—clean bowling E. I. Austen for 5.

NSW had earlier declared at the mammoth total of 6 for 710, young Don Bradman smacking an unbeaten 340. Victoria replied with 265 and 7 for 510 to draw the match but NSW won the Sheffield Shield for securing more points.

Hooker, a no. 11 bat, had distinguished himself as a batsman in NSW's previous match against Victoria on the MCG in December 1928. He stoutly defended for 304 minutes to score 62 runs and was engaged in a world record tenth-wicket partnership of 307 runs with the elegant Alan Kippax (260 not out in 387 minutes, hitting 30 fours). Thus, the self-effacing Hooker had the unique dual distinction of establishing a world record for 10th wicket (which still stands) and becoming the first and only bowler to take 4 in 4 in Sheffield Shield— all in space of one month.

Alan Walker was a versatile sportsman who played cricket and rugby at international level. As a fast left-arm bowler, he represented NSW, Australia and Nottinghamshire. He performed a hat-trick in his first season for NSW, against Queensland in the Sheffield Shield, and headed the bowling averages. For Nottinghamshire against Leicestershire in 1955 he achieved a unique top hat-trick, taking a wicket with the last ball of the first innings and wickets with the first three balls of the second.

Leg-spinner John Cassimar Treanor took a hat-trick in his first-class debut. Not selected in the original NSW team against Queensland in Brisbane in 1954-55, he came in as a last-minute replacement for the injured Test great Alan Davidson. Grabbing this opportunity, he took 5 for 146 and 3 for 59 (including the hat-trick) in a marvellous debut.

There have been quite a few instances of bowlers taking hat-tricks in their first-class debuts. The first one was by Harry Hay, a fast bowler from South Australia with a swinging action. Against Lord Hawke's England XI at Valley Oval, Unley, Adelaide, on 30 March 1903, Hay, 29, was called in to replace an injured player H. P.

Kirkwood. In a sensational dream debut, he captured 9 for 67 including an all-bowled hat-trick; his victims were C. J. Burnup, F. L. Faine and T. L. Taylor. Later he removed 'Plum' Warner and B. J. J. Bosanquet—well-known names—with successive balls.

The list of eight bowlers to perform a hat-trick on first-class debut includes as many as five from India: Vasant Ranjane in 1956-57, Joginder Singh Rao in 1963-64, Salil Ankola in 1988-89, Javagal Srinath (who later played Test cricket), and Saradindu Mukherjee in 1989-90. For details see Appendix.

Rao's debut hat-trick in 1963-64 was followed by two more in his next match, to be detailed later on.

For Border v. Eastern Province at Port Elizabeth, South Africa, in 1939-40, R. R. Phillips took a hat-trick in his *first over* in first-class cricket. However, he had played in four matches previously without bowling.

Anthony Piggott, a 20-year-old tall bowler with lively pace, took an unusual hat-trick for Sussex v. Surrey at Hove in 1978. He sent back Test cricketers Intikhab Alam, Robin Jackman and Pat Pocock to make Surrey flounder at 8 for 93. What made Piggot's hat-trick so memorable was that he had not previously taken a wicket in first-class cricket. Later, in 1983-84, he played one Test for England.

A remarkable double hat-trick was performed by Australia's Albert Trott, a tragic figure despite his exceptional talents. In three Tests for Australia he had a phenomenal batting average of 102.5. Despite scoring 38 and 72, remaining unbeaten both times, and taking 8 for 43 in the Adelaide Test of 1894-95, followed by an unbeaten 85 in the Sydney Test, he was omitted from the 1896 Australian team to England under the captaincy of elder brother Harry Trott. Bitterly disappointed, Albert migrated to England and qualified for Middlesex.

In his benefit match for Middlesex against Somerset at Lord's in 1907, he took 4 in 4 and then finished the game early by taking a hat-trick a second time in the same innings. By doing so he deprived himself of a full day's gate money. His wry comment was that he was playing himself into penury. Plagued by ill-health, loss of form and acute financial problems, he shot himself through the head at his lodgings at Willesden Green. Apart from his bowling, Trott was a magnificent hitter, and some of his towering sixes were recalled with awe for many years.

Six other bowlers have performed double hat-tricks. They are Alfred Shaw for Nottinghamshire in 1884, Jimmy Matthews for Australia in the Manchester Test of 1912, Charlie Parker for Gloucestershire in 1924, 'Roley' Jenkins for Worcestershire in 1949, Joginder Singh Rao for Services (India) in 1963-64 and Amin Lakhani for Combined XI (Pakistan) in 1978-79.

For Gloucestershire v. Notts at Trent Bridge in 1884, Alfred Shaw followed a hat-trick by taking three wickets in four balls. Not content with this, he performed the hat-trick again in the second innings. No other cricketer has come so near to achieving *three* hat-tricks in a first-class match. Shaw's bowling figures were astonishing: 41-24-29-8 and 38-23-36-6 and he bowled unchanged.

Ronald Jenkins' double hat-trick on 30 August 1949 borders on the fantastic. For Worcestershire v. Surrey at Worcester, Jenkins, a leg-break and googly bowler, performed hat-tricks in both innings. What sets aside Jenkins' feat is how his hat-trick in the second innings transformed the results of the match. Set 207 to win, Surrey began well to make 4 for 107.

At this stage Jenkins struck, and with the collaboration of Richard Howorth from the other end dismissed the last six batsmen without conceding a run. Surrey crashed from 4 for 107 to 107 all out. Jenkins' last two victims, Alec Bedser and Stuart Surridge, were both caught and bowled for ducks and he finished with match-winning figures of 6 for 112 and 5 for 54.

Coincidentally, he had also performed a hat-trick against Surrey the previous season at The Oval.

Rao's performance was also noteworthy. He started off by claiming 6 for 24 (including a hat-trick) in his first-class debut for Services against Jammu and Kashmir at Delhi in 1963-64 and pocketed two more in the same *innings* in his next match against Northern Punjab in Amritsar. Thus he holds a record for performing three hat-tricks in his first two Ranji Trophy matches. After this stranger-than-fiction start, his cricket career was cut short, but he made a name for himself as a paratrooper in Indo-Pakistan wars in 1965 and 1971. He later represented India as an amateur golfer. Major-General J. S. Rao, VSM, died in 1994, aged 56.

Fred Trueman—fast, furious and funny—came near a unique double hat-trick for Yorkshire v. Nottinghamshire at Scarborough in

1955. He dismissed R. J. Giles, F. W. Stocks and C. J. Poole off successive balls in the first innings. In the second innings, he again removed Giles and Stocks in two balls and Poole had the unenviable experience of coming in again to avoid a fiery Fred hat-trick. Amid thunderous appeals from 11 Yorkshiremen and many spectators, the ball struck Poole on the pads. After some deliberation, umpire Corrall declared him not-out which robbed Trueman of a *déjà vu* hat-trick.

Although no bowler has taken five wickets in five balls in first-class cricket, Gloucestershire's left-arm spinner Charlie Parker came very close to it, only a no-ball thwarting this phenomenon. Against Yorkshire at Bristol in his benefit match in 1922, he actually hit the stumps five times with consecutive balls, but the second ball was a no-ball. Umpires have no sense of history! Parker's final analysis was 9 for 36 (six bowled and two lbw). Despite such a spell, Gloucestershire lost the match.

South African W. A. Henderson was also a ball away from such unachievable glory. He obtained five wickets in the course of six balls for N.E. Transvaal against Orange Free State in 1937-38 at Bloemfontein. Only a season ago, Englishman W. H. Copson had performed a similar feat for Derbyshire against Warwickshire at Derby but not all his wickets were taken in the same innings. He ended the Warwickshire first innings by clean-bowling the last four batsmen, and then took a wicket with his second ball in the second innings.

The latest in this elite list (5 in 6) is Surrey's off-break bowler Pat Pocock who played 25 Tests for England. For Surrey against Sussex on 15 August 1972, he captured 4 in 4, then 5 in 6 (equalling the world record of Copson and Henderson), 6 in 9 (a world record) and 7 in 11 (another world record).

This topsy-turvy Surrey v. Sussex match at Eastbourne, Sussex, was one of the most dramatic seen in recent years, Pocock climaxing it with his magical two overs. The match started on a bleak, gloomy Saturday when only 13 overs could be bowled, Surrey being 38 without loss. On day two, a sunny Monday, Surrey declared at 4-300 and Sussex were 3-110; and a boring draw was on the cards.

But on the final day, a tense, suspenseful Tuesday, the game was set alight by two sporting declarations. Set 205 runs to win in 135 minutes, Sussex appeared in command at 1 for 187, needing only 18 runs to win in 18 balls, with Geoff Greenidge (68 not out) and Roger

Prideaux (92 not out) in tremendous form; the latter having hit 106 in the first innings.

Then came the Pocock magic. His first ball bowled Greenidge. After a dot ball, he bowled Michael Buss. Jim Parks got two from the next ball but was caught and bowled from the last. Sussex from a high of 1 for 187 were now 4 for 189, needing 16 runs to win in 12 balls. They all but sealed victory in Robin Jackman's next over, 11 runs coming with a 4, single and a 6. Sussex 4 for 200.

Only five runs to win in the last over and six wickets in hand; Prideaux 97 not out and on strike.

First ball of Pocock's last over and Prideaux anxious to reach his century (his second of the match) and win the match, skied the first ball, Jackman got under it and held it as spectators held their breath. The batsmen had crossed over. Pocock, now on a hat-trick, bowled to M. G. Griffith who had smacked a six the previous over. He hit the ball hard but was caught by R. M. Lewis. Pocock got his hat-trick and Sussex were 6 for 200, still needing five runs from four balls with four wickets remaining.

J. D. Morley came and went, stumped by Arnold Long, Pocock had 4 in 4 balls and 6 in 9 and Sussex in a panic at 7 for 200. J. Spencer took a single from the fourth delivery but Pocock bowled Tony Buss for a duck and Sussex were 8 for 201 with one ball to go. Pocock had incredibly captured 5 in 6 and 7 in 11—a world record. The home crowd, sure of a victory fifteen minutes ago, was very subdued now.

When he bowled the last delivery, it meant he had bowled seven successive balls at seven different batsmen. Now Sussex could not lose—except for the unlikely event of a run out off a no-ball—but they needed a four to win. Could the Indian import U. C. Joshi hit one? He connected and started running, crossed for a single but when attempting a second was run out. At 9 for 202, Sussex fell three runs short of a victory and the match was drawn.

Five wickets had fallen in the final pulsating over. Pocock's last two overs were recorded in the scorebook as W0W20W and WWW1W1. He had the sensational analysis of 2-0-4-7 plus a run-out at the end. 'It was the most dramatic burst of wicket-taking that first-class cricket has known, made all the more unbelievable by Pocock's analysis before the start of his penultimate over, which read 14-1-63-0,' Andrew Ward wrote in *Cricket's Strangest Matches*.

8

The Cobden Sensation

A hat-trick is like a sensual short story;
it starts with foreplay, has a gasping middle
and a throbbing climax.

There have been many and varied hat-tricks; the most common one being 'three strikes and youse are in'—all over in five minutes. Or they could be prolonged ones like those by Merv Hughes and Courtney Walsh—stretching over two days. And there is the 'journey not the destination' variety where the bowler gets obsessed and does not stop at three but wants more!

The more interesting are the freaky ones when all three batsmen are bowled or adjudged leg-before, caught by the same fielder or—weirdest of them all—stumped. How three batsmen can jump out of the crease off successive balls and perform the cricketing equivalent of Harakiri or mass suicide is beyond me.

Yet it has happened, although only once in first-class cricket. In 1893, Gloucestershire's C. L. Townsend, then aged 16, had three Somerset batsmen stumped by W. H. Brain off consecutive balls at Cheltenham. It is recorded in the scorebook as:

A. B. Newton st. Brain b. Townsend 4
G. B. Nichols st. Brain b. Townsend 0
E. J. Tyler st. Brain b. Townsend 0

There have been two instances of all three batsmen being caught by the same fielder other than the wicket-keeper in three balls. In Birmingham in 1914, G. J. Thomson of Northamptonshire, fielding at short-slip, held catches of three Warwickshire batsmen (C. S. Baker, A. W. Foster and H. Howell) in three deliveries from the bowling of S. G. Smith. Smith went on to dismiss the next man first ball, but without Thomson's assistance.

Similarly, Cyril Whites of Border assisted in an all-caught hat-trick off R. Beesly against Griqualand West at Queenstown in South Africa in 1946-47.

For Gloucestershire v. Surrey at The Oval, in September 1986, wicket-keeper R. C. (Jack) Russell caught Alex Stewart for 3, skipper A. R. Butcher for 2 and M. A. Lynch for 0 in three successive balls— off two balls from D. V. Lawrence and a ball from Courtney Walsh. Technically not a hat-trick, it was a high quality performance as Surrey lost their first three men with only five runs on the board. Earlier, Russell had top-scored in the first innings.

The only wicket-keeper to perform a 'snicky' hat-trick was Derbyshire's G. O. Dawkes who accepted three catches in three balls from Worcestershire batsmen off the bowling of H. L. Jackson at Kidderminster in 1958.

Kharshed R. Meher-Homji, with one Test appearance to his name (India v. England at Old Trafford, Manchester in 1936), was also involved in a wicket-keeper's hat-trick 27 years before Dawkes. This was for Freelooters against Railways in the semi-final of Moin-ud-Dowlah tournament in Secunderabad, India, on 1 December 1931. In three successive deliveries from fast bowler L. Ramji, a Test cricketer, keeper Meher-Homji caught Ganesh Rao, Himayatullah and Amin. The crowd exploded as this was the first instance of an all-caught-behind hat-trick in the world.

Unfortunately, this feat is not recognised in *Wisden* as only the final is given first-class status. It may be added that the quality of the players in this particular match was indeed high, with Test cricketers Vijay Merchant, Mushtaq Ali, Nazir Ali, Soli Colah, besides Ramji and Meher-Homji. As Merchant—India's all-time great batsman— later explained to *Wisden*: 'in the Moin-ud-Dowlah matches of those years, the cream of Indian talent participated and even Sir Jack Hobbs, Herbert Sutcliffe and Sir Learie Constantine took part'.

The following six bowlers have performed the 'all lbw' hat-tricks:
–H. Fisher, Yorkshire v. Somerset, Sheffield, 1932;
–J. A. Flavell, Worcestershire v. Lancashire, Manchester, 1963;
–M. J. Procter, Gloucestershire v. Essex, Westcliff, 1972;
–B. J. Ikin, Griqualand West v. OFS, Kimberley, 1973-74;
–M. J. Procter, Gloucestershire v. Yorkshire, Cheltenham, 1979;
–Aamer Wasim, Zone C. v. Lahore, Lahore, 1985-86

When praising the bowler for such enchanted (all lbw) hat-tricks, let us not bypass the mental turmoil of the umpire. When Fisher appealed for the third lbw in three balls, umpire Alec Skelding looked meditatingly down the pitch and said, 'As sure as God is my judge, that's out', and lifted his finger.

Mike Procter, the great all-rounder from South Africa, apart from taking an all lbw hat-trick also scored a century in the same match in 1979. In fact, he is the only one to achieve the all-rounder's hat-trick (a century and a hat-trick in the same match) on two occasions. Of the 10 to have done so once, Australia's master all-rounder George Giffen was the pioneer, scoring 13 and 113 and capturing 6 for 55 including the hat-trick for the touring Australians against Lancashire at Manchester in 1884.

The following year, W. E. Roller performed the unique feat of making a double century and a hat-trick for Surrey v. Sussex at The Oval. Cricketers with the dual distinctions of a 'ton 'n' trick' in the same match are listed in the Appendix. Procter is also one of six to take a hat-trick and score two fifties in a match (see Appendix).

Ten years before Giffen, W. G. Grace (MCC v. Kent at Canterbury, 1874) had scored 123 and taken 5 for 82 and 6 for 47 (including a hat-trick). But being a 12-a-side match, it is not given first-class status.

Far Left: There was a 'hat-trick' of hat-tricks in the 1928-29 Sheffield Shield season when H. I. Ebeling, Hal Hooker and Clarrie Grimmett (pictured) performed hat-tricks. *Centre:* George Giffen, the great Australian all-rounder, was the first to score a century and take a hat-trick in the same first-class match in 1884. *This page:* Larger than life-size, Bill Armstrong was the first player to take a hat-trick in the same first-class match in 1884.

(Jack Pollard Collection)

No list of dramatic hat-tricks can be complete without a mention of Fred Spofforth. His hat-trick for the touring Australians against MCC at Lord's on 27 May 1878, is still regarded with awe.

It was the second match of the tour and an expectant crowd of about 1000 had turned up to watch the colonials get humiliated. But in a sensational day's play lasting barely four and a half hours, MCC lost by 9 wickets; MCC 33 and 19, Australians 41 and 1 for 12—a match aggregate of 105.

W. G. Grace fell for 4 and Clem Booth for 0. With the score at 2 for 5, captain Dave Gregory let Spofforth loose on the English lions. In 23 balls, he captured 6 for 4—including a hat-trick with the first three balls of his fifth over which removed G. G. Hearne, Alfred Shaw and attacking batsman G. F. Vernon for ducks—the last two stumped by Billy Murdoch.

Trailing Australia by eight runs, MCC fared even worse in the second innings—being bundled out for 19. Spofforth was near another hat-trick; clean-bowling Grace for 0 with the second ball after he was dropped off the first ball. This inspired *Punch* magazine to compose a poem:

Our Grace before dinner was very soon done,
And Grace after dinner did not get a run.

With his third ball, Spofforth dismissed A. J. Webb but Booth survived to thwart hat-trick number two.

Thus, there have been many remarkable and unusual hat-tricks but none can quite match Cobden's famous hat-trick of 1870. Frank Carroll Cobden (1849-1932) 'was the hero of perhaps the most sensational piece of bowling in the history of cricket', wrote *Wisden*.

It was achieved in an Inter-Varsity match for Cambridge against Oxford at Lord's. Batting first Cambridge totalled 147 and Oxford replied with 175. Cambridge were in trouble in the second innings losing 5 for 40 (that is, only 12 runs on) but were rescued by William Yardley's scintillating 100, the first ever century in Varsity cricket. They totalled 206 and set Oxford 179 to win.

Indian all-rounder Rusi Surti is the first bowler to take a hat-trick for Queensland in the Sheffield Shield. *(Rusi Surti)*

India's Chetan Sharma performs the only hat-trick in a World Cup match when he clean bowls three New Zealanders in Nagpur in 1987.

(Supplied by B. B. Mama)

Oxford were 7 for 175 and needed only four runs to win when fast-medium bowler Cobden began his over to remember. The first ball was hit by F. H. Hill for a single. It would have gone for a four to make Oxford victorious but the stroke was brilliantly fielded by mid-wicket. Hill, a competent bat, was to remain frustratingly near the bowler as wickets tumbled at the other end.

S. E. Butler came and went, caught off the first ball he received by Bourne. Score 8 for 176, still three runs needed for the victory song. In walked T. H. Belcher, 'rather pale, but with a jaunty air which concealed a sickly feeling of nervousness', wrote The Hon. R. H. Lyttelton in *Cricket Stories*.

In dead silence, Cobden bowled a fast one well up to the batsman's legs. A vision of the winning hit flashed across Belcher's bemused mind and he raised his bat to hit the ball hard and far but missed it and was bowled off his legs. He walked away, a broken man, amid an uproarious storm of cheers from the Cambridge supporters. Score stood at 9 for 176, still three short of a win and Cobden on a hat-trick.

Last man W. A. Stewart, an excellent wicket-keeper but a poor batsman, dragged himself in as if in a trance, his ears full of dos and don'ts from just about everyone. All he had to do was to block the ball and then Hill—feeling as desperate as a blaring fire-engine caught in a traffic jam—would take over. Oxford captain Mr Pauncefote had earnestly entreated Stewart to put the bat straight in the block-hole and keep it there without moving it.

This was the scenario as you can imagine it 125 year later. Stewart standing manfully, a shiver down his spine and a dead bat on the block-hole as Cobden delivers his final ball watched by a crowd turned speechless.

Over to Lyttelton: 'Whiz went the ball; but alas!—as many other people, cricketers and politicians alike, have done—the good advice is neglected, and Stewart, instead of following his captain's exhortation to keep his bat still and upright in the block-hole, lifted it just a wee bit and fly went the bails'. And Cambridge won the cliffhanger by two runs!

'The situation was bewildering. Nobody could quite realise what had happened for a second or so, but then—up went Mr Absalom's hat, down the pavilion steps with miraculous rapidity flew the Rev. A. R. Ward, and smash went Mr Charles Marsham's umbrella against the pavilion brickwork.'

Cobden stood nearly 180 cm tall and weighed 76 kg. He was an accurate fast round-arm bowler, a free and powerful hitter who generally fielded at mid-on. He did not play for a county—let alone Test cricket—but has become a cult figure for just one dramatic over bowled 125 years ago.

9

Vanishing Tricks

If three wickets from successive deliveries
is worth a hat, then Boyle's display
deserves a full suit of clothes.
—**Francis Erskine Allan**

The feats of hat-trickers described in previous chapters appear pale in comparison when we move down to minor (non-first-class) level where sky is the limit and 9 in 9 (nine-wickets-in-nine-balls) the king.

The super sensational bowling achievements are performed at non-first-class (junior, club, school, under-16) levels played on inferior pitches, in absence of sightscreens, while most of the victims are prize 'rabbits'.

In Test cricket, the best hat-trick sequence has been four wickets in five balls by Maurice Allom. And the best in first-class cricket is 4 in 4 with Charlie Parker coming close to 5 in 5—give and take a no-ball.

However, in minor cricket you have mind-boggling figures of 7 in 7, 8 in 8—even 9 in 9, *twice*. At least three bowlers have taken three hat-tricks in a match and one, W. Clarke, *five* in a match! Now let us detail such Ripleyesque feats one by one.

High on the list of the most astonishing performance was one by a 14-year-old New Zealand schoolboy, Stephen Fleming, in December 1967. In a two innings match against Bohally Intermediate School at Blenheim, Fleming from Marlborough College A achieved the phenomenal match analysis of 1.1 eight-ball overs, 1 maiden, 9 wickets for no runs. Incredibly, he bowled nine balls in the match and captured a wicket with each delivery.

Batting first, Bohally were 9 for 17 when Fleming was given the bowling. He took a wicket with his first ball to close the Bohally innings for a paltry 17. His team declared at 9 for 45, a lead of 28.

Fleming was given the first over and what an over! He collected a wicket with each ball of the eight-ball over and Bohally were an embarrassing eight down for none. In the second over, they managed one run off the bat and two byes. Whether Fleming would have gone on to 10 in 10 or 11 in 11, we will never know. His captain—in a chivalrous mood or perhaps wishing not to risk perfection—changed Fleming and gave the ball to Graham Holdaway who had taken a hat-trick in the first innings. Holdaway polished off the remaining two batsmen in five balls and Bohally were shot out for a 'grand total' of 3 in 21 balls to lose by an innings and 25 runs.

Fleming's feat of 9 in 9—although awe-inspiring—was not unique, such is the marvel of minor cricket. In February 1931, in a school match in South Africa, left-arm bowler Paul Hugo took all 10 wickets for 3 runs. Nine of his wickets were taken with successive balls for Smithfield v. Alwal North.

There have been at least four recorded instances of bowlers dismissing 8 victims in 8 balls: These are by J. Walker for Ashcomb Park v. Tunstall in Straffordshire, 1882; by J. Stebbing for Frinsby v. Rainham in Kent, 1902; by Private J. Leake for 9th Brigade Canadian Expeditionary Force v. Canadian Army Services Corps in France in 1917; and by S. Vunisakiki for Lomalona v. HMS Leith at Suva, Fiji in 1939-40.

Leake went on to capture all 10 wickets in 12 balls.

In August 1891, W. C. Hall, a station-master, took 9 wickets in 10 balls—including 5 in a row—for Parson Drove v. Gedney Hills (Cambs) to dismiss the latter for 7. Hall's analysis was 2-1-2-9.

At least 19 bowlers have taken 7 in 7. The first one to achieve this was S. M. J. Woods (1867-1931) who played three Tests each for Australia and England, besides representing Cambridge University and Somerset. When at Royston College in 1883, he took 7 in 7. The next year Private Bone repeated this performance in a Services match in Bangalore, India.

The first one to achieve 7 in 7 in Australia was F. Howett in South Australia in 1884-85. The others to repeat this feat down-under have been J. J. Dowd at Bathurst in 1900-01, P. Mossman for Prep School v. Sydney Cape Grammar 2nd XI in 1908 -09, Malcom Perryman for Mosman District v. Neutral Bay League in B grade in a Northern Suburbs Junior Competition at Cammeray Park, Sydney in 1947-48, and by S. Harding for Wagga Wagga v. Turvey Park at Wagga, NSW, in 1972-73.

Among others to bag 7 in 7 in England are E. C. Hoddincott for Elverscreech v. King's School, Bruton, 1939, to win the match and T. J. Barson in an Under-15 match at Clifton in 1968. Ken Maxwell took 10 wickets for one run in 14 balls—including 7 in 7—for Marchington v. Trentside on 5 May 1985.

Shaun Wilson, 19, took 9 wickets in 12 balls (including 7 in 7) for Essex Club Elsenham v. White Horse, Haslow, in 1987. The latter collapsed from 0 for 12 to 12 all out, Wilson's final analysis being 6.4-5-1-9. Jonathan Pool of Harrow's School Under-15 XI also took 9 for 1 the same year. His first eight victims were bowled and he performed two hat-tricks.

Malcolm Perryman's 7 in 7 is well-documented in *The Australian Cricket* of 21 November 1947. A fastish off-spinner and former Mosman first-grader, he took all 10 wickets for six runs without assistance from fielders (nine of his victims were bowled and one was lbw). In his second over he trapped a batsman leg before off the eighth ball. Inspired, he performed the double hat-trick with the first six balls of his next over to get his cherished 7 in 7. He took three more wickets for one run in his fifth over, missing his third hat-trick when a catch was dropped. The last nine batsmen were bowled.

This was the second time he had taken all 10 in an innings, having dismissed Paddington Shire team in 1936 with a 10 for 32 haul.

Harry Boyle (1847-1907), who played 12 Tests for Australia, took 7 wickets in 8 balls for Australians v. 18 of Elland at Leeds in 1878. 'If three wickets from successive deliveries was worth a hat, then Boyle's display deserved a full suit of clothes,' commented team-mate Francis Allan. Boyle dispatched batsmen to the pavilion so quickly that later batsmen had trouble padding up fast enough to go to the middle. Impatient spectators yelled: 'Send in a man'. Another hollered in response: 'Send in three or four; one's no use!'

There are many instances of double hat-tricks (6 in 6); probably the first was by fast bowler John Wisden (later of *Wisden* fame) for England v. 22 of USA and Canada at Rochester, New York, in 1859. At least two Australians have done the double hat-trick, P. O'Shea and W. Rigg—both in 1933. O'Shea clean bowled all six batsmen.

Gerald Ziehl, a Rhodesian all-rounder, took six wickets in an over on 19 March 1952 at Salisbury. Playing for Stainton, near Penrith, in England, Brian Hill, aged 16, dismissed six Staffield batsmen with six successive balls, four in one over and two in the next. But the year of this achievement is not mentioned in my source, *This Curious Game of Cricket* by George Mell.

Ben Sangster, 12, from Holmwood Preparatory School near Liverpool in England bowled six batsmen from Lytham School in six balls in 1975. In a Shrewsbury School Under-16 match, J. C. Yeoward also bowled 6 in 6 in 1948.

According to *Gillette Book of Records*, Ron Winfield of City Transport XI was put on to bowl with Nottingham XI's score at 3 for 39. He claimed 6 in 6 and caught the last man off the first ball of the other bowler and Notts plummeted to 39 all out—losing seven wickets in seven balls; seven ducks quacking in unison!

Next best is 6 in 7 by Kevin Sobels, a medium-pacer for Muswellbrook Workers, Scone v. Senenhoe ABC Bunnen United in 1976. He might have had 7 in 7 but an lbw appeal was turned down.

There have been numerous instances of 5 in 5: Oxford University's A. Cazenove being probably the first to do so in 1853. The most curious 5 in 5 was achieved by Noel Jones on his birthday, on 25 December 1947. It was for Yale Logs v. Noel Burnett's XI at Preston Park, Brighton (England)—a cause for triple celebration; Noel, Noel! In 1993, Leigh Atkinson, a second cousin of Graham Gooch, took 5 in 5 in a club match for Flackwell Heath.

D. B. Tapia of Independent Parsee Club, Bombay, in 1889 and J. S. Warden at Calcutta in 1920 also captured 5 in 5, but Private Osborne's 5 in 5 for the Duke of Wellington's Regiment v. Gezira Cricket Club at Gezira, Egypt, in 1925 deserves special mention.

It happened in an important match as the Gezira CC, the so-called MCC of Egypt, had selected their strongest side. They batted first and were going well when Osborne changed ends to get the advantage of breeze behind him. At 2 for 92, he bowled C. Hartopp for one. His next delivery hit the middle stump of R. E. More, their captain and recognised as the best cricketer in Egypt (also an old Oxford Blue and a well-known Middlesex amateur). Osborne's next two balls clean bowled Captain Dobbie and Lieutenant J. B. J. Hankey for ducks. His fifth ball trapped Colonel J. B. Wells—one of their soundest batsmen—lbw.

Thus Osborne, a young soldier, had captured 5 in 5 without the assistance of a fielder in his first major (although non first-class) match, and finished with 7 for 37.

Former Australian Test all-rounder Gary Gilmour (483 runs and 54 wickets in 15 Tests) had his magical moment for Western Suburbs v. Gordon in the semi-final of Sydney's first-grade competition in 1972-73. Having demolished Gordon in the previous season's final by taking 10 for 27, left-handed Gilmour was pumped up for more.

Defending a total of 340, Gilmour took a wicket in each of his first two overs to have Gordon gasping at 3 for 6. Then NSW opener Marshall Rosen and Brian Thomson put on 154 runs for the fourth wicket, cutting a wayward Gilmour to size. At the right time, Western Suburbs captain Bob Simpson brought Gilmour back into the attack half an hour before lunch on the second day.

Off the first ball of his second over, Gilmour had the well-set Thomson caught behind by Col Rowe for 51, then had Corben caught at first slip by Simpson and completed the hat-trick by bowling McKaughan next ball. With his fourth delivery, he had Thomas caught in the slip by Frank Teager. Thus, in four balls, Gilmour turned the match full-circle, as Gordon collapsed from 3 for 160 to 7 for 160 and lost. Wests went on to defeat Balmain in the final to win consecutive championships.

At least seven bowlers have taken all 20 wickets in junior matches, Fred Spofforth—that man again!—being the first in 1881-82 at Bendigo, Victoria, but that performance did not include a hat-trick. In 1932, Y. S. Ramaswamy, aged 18, for Marimallapa High School v. Wesleyan High School, Bangalore, took 20 for 31 including a hat-trick—bowling leg-breaks and googlies.

Lou Benaud, Richie's father, took all 20 in a match for Penrith Waratah v. St Mary's, NSW in 1922-23; 10 for 30 in the first innings (which included 4 in 4) and 10 for 35 in the second.

Now to hat-tricks in tandem when two bowlers have performed one in successive overs. For Young Zoroastrian Club v. Parsee Gymkhana in Bombay in 1899, D. P. Banaji took 4 in 4. In the very next over, D. N. Writer performed a hat-trick.

In 1972, two Australian bowlers combined to produce a procession of seven departing batsmen in a second-grade match between Lake Illawarra and Gerringong. First, Gerringong's David Emery took a wicket with each of the last three balls of his over. From the other end Brian Arberry dismissed four batsmen with consecutive balls, and Lake Illawarra tumbled from 2 for 30 to 9 for 30.

Still on the tandem theme but with a difference, two bowlers from the same club each achieved a hat-trick on 19 June 1983, but in different matches. Playing for Botany Bay, Middlesex v. Edmonton, Jonathon Elliot took a hat-trick and followed it up with 102 not out (studded with nine sixes) which enabled his team to win by one wicket. On the same day, for Botany Bay's 2nd XI v. Winchester Hill at Ford's Grove, Brian Chetwynd also took a hat-trick.

In a memorable match between Parsees and Secunderabad in Bombay in 1891, the former won with only two minutes to spare—thanks to their captain Dr Mehelashah Pavri's awesome spell reminiscent of Frank Cobden's celebrated hat-trick of 1870. In reply to Parsee's 69, Secunderabad scored 65, Pavri's analysis being 10-9-1-3. Parsees declared their second innings closed at 6-131, challenging their opponents to score 136 runs in 75 minutes.

At 6 for 43, Pavri began what turned out to be the final over. The opposition needed an impossible 96 runs in under ten minutes. So confident were they of a draw, that some of their batsmen went off to play tennis.

Pavri, India's first top-notch cricketer who later played for Middlesex, thought differently. A brainy fast-medium bowler, he clean bowled the last four batsmen Dewling, Trevlin, Captain Stevens and Shute. Some of them had to change from tennis shorts to cricket flannels like firemen. Parsees snatched a 97 run shock victory with two minutes remaining.

'The standard of cricket was fairly high and the excitement among the spectators was beyond bounds,' Pavri recalled.

With such abundance of riches, it is interesting to speculate as to who should wear the crown for being the champion hat-tricker in minor cricket. It will be hard to go past the Kiwi teenager Stephen Fleming. He bowled nine balls in a match and took a wicket with *each* ball. Even assuming that the standard of batting was deplorable, the odds of this ever happening again would be astronomical. Imagine, a wicket a ball, nine times, each ball claiming a wicket! This is not just a world record, it is perfection personified. Now, who will be the runner-up?

Aircraftsman Monks in 1931 took three hat-tricks in a match for RAF v. The Army Club in Cairo. He performed a hat-trick and later bowled 4 in 4 in the first innings. In the second innings, he completed the third hat-trick of the match and subsequently bowled the last two batsmen with consecutive balls, thus coming close to his fourth hat-trick!

Unique? Not quite. Gordon Neal had made headlines in a country match in Queensland in 1892-93 by taking 10 for 5—including three hat-tricks. And M. F. McConnell took three hat-tricks in an innings for Loxton House v. Bronston House, Oundle, on 27 June 1939.

Now to my personal choice of the runner-up. In Kent, W. Clarke (any relation of Superman?) performed *five* hat-tricks for St Augustine's College, Ashford v. Ashford Church Choir in 1912. He achieved three hat-tricks in the first innings and two in the second.

'His appetite for hat-tricks was insatiable,' wrote Harvey Day, an expert on minor cricket records.

A delighted Trevor Kidd, 12, after clean-bowling six batsmen in six balls for St Martins School v. Marian College in Johannesburg. *(Jonty Winch)*

10
Tall Tales and True

To the non-cricketing person, hat-tricks are
moments in time. To the cognoscente, they
are milestones of personal triumph.
— Tony Matchett

TIME MACHINE
The first bowler to dismiss four batsmen in four balls was J. Wells, the father of well-known novelist H. G. Wells. J. Wells' 4 in 4 was for Kent against Sussex at Brighton in 1862.

PLAY ON CRICKET
Thomas Browne's play *The Hat-Trick* had a heroine who was modelled on Rachel Heyhoe-Flint, the former captain of England in women's cricket.

RIGHT ROYAL HAT-TRICK
King George VI was not just a cricket lover. In his younger days, when Prince Albert, he was a talented left-handed all-rounder. *Wisden 1952* mentions that once he bowled King Edward VII, King George V and the Duke of Windsor with successive deliveries. There is a ball mounted in the mess-room of the Royal Navy College, Dartmouth, commemorating this feat on the private ground at Windsor Castle.

MAJOR HAT-TRICK
When 12, England's Prime Minister John Major won the Best Young Cricketer of the Year award from London's *Evening Standard* after taking 7 for 9—including a hat-trick—in a school match.

CAPTAIN'S DUNCE CAP

When playing for St Ives Under-16 for Hornsby-Ku-Ring-Gai Competition at Hassel Park in Sydney in 1982, Alex McKay was on a hat-trick. Their captain, Dave Proverst, warned his team: 'If anyone drops a catch to rob Alex of his hat-trick, he will be dropped next Saturday,' narrates John Wright, a stylish all-rounder for Hornsby RSL Club, and not the New Zealand Test opener.

'Came the third ball, the nervous batsman skied a catch and was dropped by, guess who, the red-faced Dave Proverst!' John added with a wicked smile.

AMBIDEXTROUS TRICK

In 1947, E. F. Mellor took a hat-trick for his home village of Perry St v. Axminster in the UK. He repeated the feat the following year for Perry St v. Forton. The only difference was that in 1947 he bowled left-handed and in 1948 right-handed.

MOTHERS OF 'HAT-TRICK'

Tall and hefty Baqa Jilani performed the first hat-trick in Ranji Trophy in India. For Northern India against Southern Punjab (all out for 22) he took 5 for 7 in 25 balls—including the pioneering hat-trick in 1934-35. All his three hat-trick victims were Sikhs (those who wear turbans and usually have the same surname Singh).

A right-arm fast-medium bowler and useful lower order batsman, Jilani toured England with the Indian team in 1936. He played his only Test at The Oval in 1936 without achieving much.

How Jilani was included in that Test makes an interesting story. The Indian team of 1930s was full of dissension and their weak captain Maharajkumar of Vizianagram ('Vizzy' for short) drew Jilani aside and whispered: 'Insult C. K. Nayudu at the breakfast table and you're in the Test'. C. K. Nayudu was the former captain of India, a fine cricketer and the idol of cricket fans, but Jilani did as told and soon made his Test debut.

Jilani had three sisters, each of whom produced a Test captain for Pakistan: Majid Khan (son of Dr Jahangir Khan who had played four Tests for India), Javed Burki and the colourful Imran Khan.

A magistrate by profession, Jilani died in 1940, aged 29, when he fell from a balcony following an epileptic seizure.

LOOK OUT, IT'S CATCHING!

Reg Giddey, now 76, was a leg-spinner who played for Northern Districts with distinction in the 1940s. In a second grade match in 1945-46, he performed two hat-tricks at Waitara Oval, Sydney. One of these was remarkable because all three victims were caught by the *same* fielder, Phil Payne, in the first slip. Later, from 1947 to 1960, Reg played first grade for Gordon and took 452 wickets, third highest after Dick Guy and the great Charlie Macartney.

There have been very few such instances—all three batsmen being caught by the same fielder in three tantalising deliveries. But Peter Davis' hat-trick for Hammersmith Police Station v. Wellington College in Berkshire, UK, in 1983 was unique. The first victim gave him a dolly return catch. The next one smashed the ball back to him head high with tremendous power and Peter caught it. Had he not, he would have needed urgent dental surgery. With fielders converging around the batsman like vultures, Peter bowled a slower ball. This was lofted high by the batsman and T. D. Grace, fielding at short-leg, got ready to catch it. Just then Davis rushed in, pushed Grace away from the ball's flight and caught it himself to make it an extraordinary caught-and-bowled hat-trick.

Ron Johnston, currently the President of Illawarra Junior Cricket Association in NSW, had the incredible experience of playing in *two* matches in which a fielder caught three batsmen in three balls. As a student teacher in 1956, he played for Wagga Wagga Teachers School v. The Agricultural College at Gissing Oval when fast-medium bowler Ian Clacher dismissed batsmen nos 3, 4 and 5 in three balls—all caught by John Cowell at silly mid-on. Two years later, for Tarcutta v. Caraboat, three of Ron's team-mates were hat-trick victims of spinner Albert Jones, all caught at deep mid-on by brother Tom.

HAT-TRICK AT 77. . .

Andy Beatty of Fox Valley Club in Hornsby, Sydney, is 82 and still plays every Sunday as a slow leg-spinner. He was a medium-pacer till 65. In 1990, he took a hat-trick at Narromine in NSW. He was then 77.

. . . AND AT 10

Jared Splatt remembers a hat-trick his friend Johnnie 'Piwi' Dickson, aged 10, achieved for Glen Waverly Hawkes Cricket Club v.

Vermont South CC in October 1993. Piwi struck in his sixth over. To quote Jared, aged 11 and already an interesting writer: 'The first ball was a yorker which knocked middle stump right out of the ground. Piwi charged down the pitch like a bull, his monkey-like face looking triumphant. Piwi walked back to his mark, took a deep breath, muttered "down you go", ran fast and launched the ball at rocket speed. The batsman hit the ball in the air and square-leg caught it.

'Before bowling the third ball, he told me: "this delivery might be a small one for me but it's gonna be a big one in the scorebook". He ran in and everything appeared to go in slow motion. The ball went up rib high and dropped sharply. The batsman tried to hook but missed it and was bowled . . .and Piwi got his hat-trick.'

More remarkable than the hat-trick is 11-year-old Jared's colourful style of writing. 'I want to be a writer one day,' he concluded.

Ten year-old Ben Hale's description of his friend Kym Handyside's hat-trick is presented in the plate overleaf.

ST IVES BLUES

Zubin Meher-Homji, 10, achieved a rare hat-trick in the semi-final of Junior School's competition in November 1987. Playing for Davidson Park Primary School in St Ives, Sydney, against eventual champions West Pymble Primary, Zubin took three wickets without conceding a run—all three of the hat-trick victims being caught and bowled. For St Ives Blues a week before, he had captured 4 for 0 (without a hat-trick). Thus, he had taken seven wickets in consecutive matches without conceding a run.

Next year for St Ives Under-11 against Proville at Killara Oval, Sydney, on 29 October 1988, he took another hat-trick and has a mounted trophy to show for it. His grand-uncle, Kharshed R. Meher-Homji, had played one Test for India against England at Manchester in 1936 as a wicket-keeper.

Ingrid Knight, also from St Ives Blues, took 5 for 0 (all bowled—including a hat-trick) in an Under-11 match at Toolang Park, Sydney, in October 1987. A tear away fast bowler, she frightened boys away with her speed and bounce. The coincidence of the match was Ingrid facing Bergman in the opening over. She cover-drove his first ball for four but was bowled the next ball.

Dear Mr. Meher-Homji

I am writing to you after your story in the Inside Edge. I have a hat trick to share with you. It's at a school match. The hat trick takers name is Kym Handyside. He is the vice captain an all rounder, a medium fast bowler. He is coming around the wicket. The delivery I'm not so sure weather it swing in (I was fielding at cover) But it hit off-stump. The second delivery just the same hitting off stump. The third blocked and caught at a wide short leg

Yours Truly
Ben Hales

My age is 10. Kym's age is 12.

When asked whether she had heard of actress Ingrid Bergman, she replied, 'I was named after her'. But actresses were not her idols; Greg Matthews, Richard Hadlee and Rugby League players were.

HIT-TRICK

Although not a hat-trick, cricket writer Gerald Brodribb cites a curious series of dismissals in *Some Memorable Bowling*. Middlesex lost three of their first four batsmen to Kent as follows:

H. W. Lee hit wicket b. A.P. Freeman 81

R. H. Twining hit wicket b. A.P. Freeman 41

E. Hendren hit wicket b. A.P. Freeman 0

4 IN 4 AT 44

Graham Christie, the 44-year-old captain/coach of Ashwood's first XI against Glen Iris in Victoria's A-Grade match, captured four wickets in four balls on 9 October 1993. Off ball nos 2, 3, 4 and 5, he had batsmen caught, bowled, lbw and bowled. With the feeling of a man who has been blessed, Graham charged in for his last ball with a possible 5 in 5 beckoning. A huge shout of 'howzat' for lbw was put to the umpire who politely declined.

Perhaps he should wait till he is 55 for such a numerically apt feat!

UNLUCKY CHIESE

Playing for Stanmore against Radlett (England) in 1980, Ross Chiese captured five wickets in an over but without a hat-trick. His score-book entry, writes Jonathan Rice in *Curiosities of Cricket*, was WW0W nb WW (nb standing for a no ball).

5 IN 5

John Stead, now 32, took five wickets in five balls for Vaucluse Bay, Sydney v. Randwick High School in February 1978. Aged 15 then, he finished with 8 wickets for 2 runs. He later played grade cricket with Tony Greig for Waverly Club in Sydney. John shares a club record for most wickets in a season (62) with David Hourn—a Sheffield Shield player.

Austin Punch, who played 31 matches for NSW after World War I, took 192 wickets at 27.72 and scored 8632 runs at 36.78 for North Sydney Club. In 1911-12, when 17, he took 5 in 5 for the club's third-grade match.

And in February 1995, David Hirst, bowling for South East Sydney in the Shires competition against Epping, took 5 in 5, finishing with 7 for 21.

No chapter on *Tall Tales and True* can be complete without a W. G. Grace anecdote. *(Ronald Cardwell Collection)*

W. G.'S MUCH-DELAYED APPEAL

No list of cricket stories can be complete without a W. G. Grace anecdote. Eve Oxlade, originally from England, now settled in Sydney—having watched and umpired games (cricket, football, tennis, karate) in England, South Africa and Rhodesia (now Zimbabwe)—narrated this tall tale.

In the last over of the day, W.G. had dismissed two batsmen in two deliveries and hit pads of the new batsman with his next ball. But before he could appeal, the umpire rushed away in a desperate hurry to visit the toilet.

When the match resumed the next morning W.G. appealed for last evening's happening and the umpire said 'Out'.

Appears apocryphal, but then who can argue with nature?

FOR AND AGAINST

Former Kent opening bowler David Sayer took a hat-trick for Oxford University against his own county Kent at Oxford on 4 June 1958. One of his victims was English fast bowler Fred Ridgway. Oddly, Ridgway achieved a hat-trick for Kent the same afternoon.

'Two hat-tricks in the same match is unusual on its own,' writes David Priestly from Maidstone, 'but the story is completed in July 1964 when Sayer took a hat-trick playing *for* Kent against Glamorgan at Maidstone, thus achieving the rare, if not unique distinction of a hat-trick for and against his first-class club.'

7 IN 8 IN WAGGA WAGGA

AAP correspondent Ian Jessup told me this story in the SCG Press Box during the enthralling Australia v. England Test of January 1995. In 1973, his school friend Stewart Harding took 7 in 8 for Wagga Primary School in an inter-school competition in Wagga Wagga, NSW.

PARADOXICAL

Dr K. B. Orr, a leg-spinner and a surgeon, performed three hat-tricks in a cricket career extending over 50 summers. The first one was for the University of Sydney in the late 1940s, second one for Leicestershire General Hospital in the UK in the 1950s and the third one for Scots Old Boys at St Andrews College Ground in Sydney University in 1990. He remembers his 1990 hat-trick with pride because he was 65 then.

After a long wait, the captain gave him a bowl. Two of his three victims were caught by a hopeless fielder. He would have taken 4 in 4 but an excellent fielder dropped the next batsman.

MERV'S MOSMANIA

Merv Black performed four hat-tricks in Sydney Grade cricket; the first three against the same team: Mosman. His first HT was in his grade debut; for Central Cumberland v. Mosman in 1957-58 in third grade. The second was in 1974-75 for Sutherland v. Mosman in first grade and the third one in 1985-86 when playing fourth grade for Sutherland v. Mosman.

In between his second and third HTs, he bitterly regrets 'one that got away'. In the fourth-grade final in 1975, Sutherland played Mosman (again!) and Merv bowled 2 in 2. The new batsman edged his first ball and was caught by Alan Campbell, the current NSW Director of Coaching, and a State selector. But to Merv's crushing disappointment, the umpire called it a no-ball on a trivial technical hitch. The short-leg fielder had one foot on the cut portion of the wicket. Now irate, Merv clean-bowled him next ball—but no HT.

His most cherished HT was in 1986-87, when he was 49. It was again in the fourth grade final, but—surprise, surprise—against Randwick. The HT took 30 minutes to complete. Tom Iceton, a colleague of Merv, gives details: 'Merv took a wicket with the fifth ball of an over and afternoon tea (of 20 minutes duration) was taken. After tea, he completed his over by capturing a wicket with the last ball of the interrupted over. After a bowler completed an over from the other end, Merv took a wicket with the first ball of his next over.'

His namesake, Test star Merv Hughes, performed a three-over HT in the Perth Test two years later.

The remarkably durable Merv Black captured 346 first-grade wickets at 18.27 for Central Cumberland, St George and Sutherland from 1957 to 1982; and 830 scalps at 15.32 in all grades from 1957 to 1988.

HIS PRIZE—DIGESTIVE RENNIE

B. Scott, 10, performed an HT for an important school match in England during World War II. And his prize? Digestive Rennie presented by his teacher. Recalls Denise, his wife: 'Sweets were unavailable in the War years and he was very proud of his "prize" which he took home and shared with his mother. She is a very old lady now but still boasts about her son's hat-trick.'

HUNT'S 11 HTS

Left-arm medium-pacer Bill Hunt (1908-1983) made his first-class debut for NSW in 1929-30 and played his only Test (v. South Africa) in 1931-32. A rebel, he did not get on well with Australian captain Bill Woodfull and decided to play Lancashire League cricket in England. The talented Hunt took 11 HTs in his career, five of them in 1933. The rebel from Balmain mellowed in later life and spent much of his time in establishing the SCG Cricket Museum.

Left arm medium-pacer Bill Hunt took 11 hat-tricks in all types of cricket; five of them in 1933. *(Jack Pollard Collection).*

NINE HAT-TRICKS FOR FRANK

Frank Burns played 34 consecutive seasons for Wallsend District Club in Newcastle, NSW, from the mid-1940s to late 1970s. He captured over 1600 wickets—including nine HTs—in second, third and fourth grade matches, informs club secretary and statistician Jack Brown.

Frank's skipper Neville Matthews (father of Test cricketer Greg Matthews) also took two hat-tricks in successive seasons, 1960-61 and 1961-62, in the fourth grade.

Playing for the same club in the third grade, Ian Stone sent back four batsmen in five balls which included an HT; his sequence: bowled, lbw, lbw, dot, bowled.

EVERY LITTLE HELPS

It was no little achievement for Bill Mossop of Penrith's third XI. In an Eden Valley League match, Mossop clean bowled Norman Little and his nephews Ian and David Little off successive balls for ducks for an unusual HT. Not quite satisfied, Mossop trapped John Little lbw to complete the family downfall, according to *The Cricketer* (England) of November 1974.

KAPIL AT BOTH ENDS

In limited-overs internationals (LOI), India's ace all-rounder Kapil Dev took a hat-trick (v. Sri Lanka in 1990-91) and was a victim of a hat-trick by Danny Morrison of New Zealand in 1993-94.

Of the 30 HTs registered at international levels (21 in Tests and 9 in LOIs), Kapil provides the *only* instance of a cricketer at both the agony and the ecstasy ends.

PETER'S CLEAN DOUBLE TRICK

Captaining 16C Newington College, Stanmore against SCEGS (also known as 'Shore') at Northbridge Oval, Sydney, on 12 November 1994, Peter Phillips, aged 15, took six wickets without conceding a run in 15 balls. He ended Shore's innings with a magical spell of 6 in 7—including two HTs—all six being clean bowled.

Chasing 149 for a victory, Shore started confidently and were 1 for 45 in eight overs when Peter brought himself on. 'I started with a maiden over and two dot balls started my next. I then bowled three batsmen for a hat-trick. A dot ball ended the over. In my next over, I started with another hat-trick—again all bowled—and Shore was all out for a mere 49,' Peter wrote.

His figures of 2.3 overs, 2 maidens, 6 for 0 have never been matched in Newington College's long cricket history. The match ball and a copy of the scorebook are now in the College's Sports Museum.

DIFFERENT ERA

When playing fourth-grade for Sydney High School against North Sydney Boys High School in 1937, medium-pacer Val Davies, then 14, took four wickets in a row in his second over.

He was on a high and 'hungry for more' but the master-in-charge, C. P. Schrader, told him that he would not be bowling again that day 'as we have to be good sports in order to make a match of the game'.

GRAND SLAMS BY JACK AND ALLAN

It was a hard tour by the Australian Old Collegians during their Silver Jubilee World Tour in 1984. They were playing their 40th match of the tour against a Combined Sussex League XI in Sussex. Sussex were 7 for 100 when Jack Iredale, a first-grader with the Northern District Club in NSW, came in to bowl. His first ball was a loosener and the batsman whacked it. Jack threw his hand up in exasperation but the ball struck miraculously in his palm. Off his next ball, the batsman was caught at silly mid-off and then no. 11 was adjudged lbw. His team mate Geoff Coleman wrote: 'Jack had bowled three balls in the whole game and took 3 for 0'.

Allan Tegg had a similar exhilarating experience in an Under-14 match for Belmont at Broadmeadow, Newcastle, NSW, in 1967. The opponents were seven down when Allan was given the ball. His first delivery beat and bowled the batsman, his second was lifted and caught by Layne Deveridge. Now with nine fielders and wicket-keeper hovering around the last man in, a highly pumped-up Allan bowled him. 'Stumps went flying even though it appeared to happen in slow motion to me.' His figures: 0.3 over, 3 wickets for 0.

NICE AIM, BROOKS

There was a run out of hat-tricks in a match between Wanstead County High School and George Monoux Grammar School at Walthanston in England in 1962. While standing at cover, Wanstead fielder Stephen C. Brooks ran out three batsmen with three throws in three balls.

BIZARRE RECORDS

• In a Daily News Trophy match in Ceylon between Moore Sports Club and Notts Cricket and Athletic Club (year not mentioned), M. A. Wahind warned batsman no. 8 about backing up. His conscience now appeased, he 'Mankaded' batsmen nos 8, 9 and 10. A weird hat-trick of back-up run outs.

• S. M. J. (Sammy) Woods played Tests for both Australia and England from 1888 to 1895. He is still remembered for a freaky over he bowled as a schoolboy. For Brighton College in the 1880s, he bowled an over in which he hit stumps eight times in an over but was rewarded by only three wickets, and no hat-trick! He started with a hat-trick of no-balls. His fourth ball bowled a batsman. The fifth touched the leg-stump without disturbing it and went for byes. His sixth and seventh balls bowled batsmen. The eighth hit the stumps but failed to remove bails and went for four byes.

• Curry Rivel bowler Brian Rostill gave away 17 runs in his first over against Pitminster in May 1980. But his luck changed dramatically in the next over when he took six wickets—all clean bowled. In between he bowled two no balls which also hit the stumps.

(Source: *The Cricketer Book of Cricket Disasters and Bizarre Records*, Century Publishing, London, 1983.)

IN TANDEM

For Heartaches CC v. Waggoners CC at Abingdon on 22 June 1975, left-arm medium pacer and noted cricket writer Jonathan Rice took wickets off his fifth and sixth balls. The next over Chris Cliff dismissed batsmen off his first and second balls—both caught by Rice. Thus, the final four wickets had fallen in four successive balls, and two bowlers were on hat-trick but neither completed it. Rice was involved in all four dismissals—first as a bowler and then as a fielder. Despite this extraordinary dual achievement, Heartaches lost by 22 runs which probably explains their name!

A. Townsend and K. Phillips were more successful when bowling for Tamworth-in-Arden (England) against Knowle & Dorridge in 1980. Townsend took three wickets—all clean bowled—with the last three balls of his over and then Phillips sent back three bats, also clean-bowled, with his first and only three balls of the next over. A chastened Knowle & Dorridge team was shot out for 15.

WHERE STEVE GOES, HAT-TRICKS FOLLOW

Steve Wiles from Midland Bank Cricket Club, Yorkshire, played five matches in which a hat-trick was performed. He played a major role in two of them. When team mate Lee Woolway (against Tinsley at Sheffield in 1990) took two wickets off successive balls at the end of an over, Steve had a gut-feeling and suggested to his skipper that he should be moved from square-leg to short-leg. The captain agreed and when Lee bowled his first ball in the next over, a catch came Steve's way and he caught it to complete the hat-trick.

The next hat-trick was taken by Steve himself in August 1993, watched by his 14-year-old son Ian, fielding at fine-leg. 'I've been dining out of this story for two years now,' Steve recalls.

18TH TIME LUCKY

Between 1958 and 1965, left-arm leg-spinner David Burke from Bexley, NSW, played for Kingsgrove High School and Kingsgrove, coming close to a hat-trick (two wickets in two balls) seventeen times.

He tried off-spin against Kingsgrove North for a change of luck. 'I bowled two victims with prodigious off-breaks. After 17 failures I was filled with negative feelings and decided to bowl another off-break. It landed on the spot and spun viciously. The batsman swung at it high to square-leg fielder Geoff Larking who held the ball high above his head. I rushed to hug him gleefully.'

David later played grade cricket for Mosman, mostly thirds, sometimes in seconds. Allan Border, he recalls, was then playing first grade as a 16-year-old.

REID'S KIWI TRICK IN SCG LIGHTS

Malcolm Groham has done scoring for Western Suburbs in Sydney for 26 seasons and occasionally at the SCG in limited-overs internationals. He 'scored' his 500th match on Australia Day, 1995. In this time he is proud to have 'scored' five hat-tricks, two of which he describes graphically.

One was by Test cricketer Gary Gilmour in the 1972-73 Sydney first grade semi-final (which is featured in the previous chapter) and the other by tall Bruce Reid for Australia v. New Zealand at the SCG on 29 January 1986 in a day-night international. Reid dismissed B. R. Blair with the sixth ball of his eighth over and then off the first two balls in his next he sent back E. B. McSweeney and S. R. Gillespie. This was only the second hat-trick in a limited-overs international (after Jalal-ud-Din's for Pakistan v. Australia at Hyderabad in 1982-83) and the first one under lights.

WAHROONGA EXPRESS

Raymond Alfred Eaton, 15, took all 10 wickets for 27 runs for Wahroonga College, Sydney, in 1908. The next season he went one better, clean bowling all 10 for 5 runs against North Sydney Grammar School. A faded clipping from *The Referee* of 1909 (sent by his son Ken) adds: 'He [Raymond] is tall and bowls at terrific pace for his age, being termed young Cotter. He also bowls a good leg and off-break ball. In addition, the lad secured the batting average for his College . . . He has now joined Barker College, Hornsby and on his first appearance for his new College against a Sydney Grammar School XI he made an auspicious start by taking three (3) wickets with his first three balls.'

'The item holds special interest and pride for me', writes Ken, now aged 72.

FROM BOTH ENDS FOR LLOYD AND TODD

Lloyd Galperin, 15, can dish it out and take it as well. For Under-16s in 1993-94, he took a hat-trick for Randwick-Botany Police Boys Club which was spread over two innings and seven days. He bowled the last two batsmen at Queens Park, Waverly, which ended the opponent's first innings. Next week, he bowled a batsman off his first ball in the second innings. He was to take two more hat-tricks, against Randwick Blue and Randwick Green.

In 1992, he was the third victim in a hat-trick sequence for South Eastern team v. Gosford at Little Bay, Malabar, NSW. This was in an important Under-14 Representative match where the standard of cricket is high. He had a broken finger then but whether that contributed to his 'instant dismissal' is something we will never know.

Todd Liston of Panania, NSW, had a similar experience. When visiting the beautiful Northern Victorian town of Corryong in 1983, his cousin asked him to play for a local team. The opponents were struggling at 7 for 48 when Todd, aged 13, was given the ball. He clean-bowled the last three men with his first three balls.

He had a contrasting experience the following season. Playing for South Broken Hill Under-15s in Broken Hill in 1984, he went in with the score at 8 for 36 and the bowler on a hat-trick. 'Being nervous, I awaited the outcome. In came the tall, left-handed paceman à la Bruce Reid. It was a blur, crunch, rattle, jubilation, despair. Off I walked, head down, in despair.'

STUMPED FOR WORDS

For Lord Wandsworth's College (Basingstoke) v. St Bartholomew (Newbury, UK), Mark Palmer performed a freaky HT in June 1994. All three of his victims were stumped by stand-in wicket-keeper Colin Walker.

10 FOR 77 AND ALL THAT

When representing Walton's Second XI v. Basingstoke (UK) in September 1994, third change bowler Peter Webb took all 10 wickets for 77, ending the match with an HT.

Alex Kelly, 17, went one better. For Bishop Auckland in a 20-overs evening match in 1994, against Newton Aycliff in the Durham County Junior League, he took all 10 wickets—all bowled—for no runs in 27 balls. 'Every time the ball left my hand the stumps seemed to fly,' Alex said.

Wisden Cricket Monthly cites two more instances of 'all for none'; Dick Usherwood's 10 for 0, all bowled, in 27 balls for St George's Harpenden Under-12 XI in 1948 and Jenning Tune's 10 for 0, all bowled, in 30 balls for Cliffe v. Eastrington in a league match in Yorkshire on 6 May 1922. Oddly, there is no mention of an HT in any of these 10 for 0 performances.

'SAME AGAIN'

For Oudtschoorn against Port Elizabeth in South Africa, Ralph Lindsay dismissed Voges, Jones and Le Grange in consecutive balls in March 1965. It must be a case of déjà vu for Ralph because in 1957 on the same ground and against the same opponents he had achieved an HT, his victims being—you guessed it—Voges, Jones and Le Grange. No wonder, the dailies headlined the story 'Same Again' in 1965.

LEG, MIDDLE AND OFF—IN A ROW

George Mell gives another gem in his *This Curious Game of Cricket*. 'At Sleaford on 20 August 1892, a Mr Aitken for the local side clean bowled three men with successive balls, each time breaking a stump in halves—the leg, middle and off-stumps respectively.'

WICKEY TURNS TRICKY

Warwickshire wicket-keeper Alan Smith exchanged a ball for his keeping gloves on 6 August 1965. He marked the occasion by performing an HT against Essex at Clacton, dismissing both the openers G. E. Barker and G. J. Smith and the no. 4 batsman Keith Fletcher, a Test cricketer. Later on he dismissed another Test cricketer Trevor Bailey for good measure to take 4 for 0 in a 34-ball spell. He finished with 21-10-36-4; not bad for a wicket-keeper.

This is not an isolated incident. India's wicket-keeper Probir Sen (20 catches and 11 stumpings in 14 Tests—including five stumpings in one Test) also once discarded gloves and bowled in a Ranji Trophy match for Bengal v. Orissa at Cuttack in 1954-55. And he shocked all—himself included—by taking an HT.

SAME BALL—TWO TRICKS

Bob Davidson, adviser to the Minister of Industry, Science and Technology, sent me this unique story. He took an HT in 1962-63 when playing for Charlestown in the Newcastle Junior Saturday afternoon Competition. The ball was handed over to the Club President Ken Goodwin to get it mounted for presentation.

Four weeks later, the club manager could not find a ball in the kit bag for a match about to start. In desperation, he took the ball off the mantelpiece and used it as a match ball. And Bob took an HT with *that* ball again.

'I still have the Trophy with the ball mounted, but unfortunately (and I was very disappointed at this then) the inscription does not even mention there were two HTs, let alone the unusual circumstances.'

Davidson played for the next 30 years in first-grade and sometimes as representative bowler in Newcastle, Canberra and NSW bush, but never managed another HT. His son, Mark, performed two HTs as junior in 1985 but 'the lucky man has *two* Trophies to show for it', writes Bob.

IS DON, IS GOOOOD!

Don Moyes of Berwick, Victoria, was almost as prolific with his HTs at district level, as *the* Don (Bradman) was with his double centuries at all levels. Moyes took seven HTs in Southern and Federal

District in Melbourne.

His first HT was in an inter-class match for his state school: then a 4 in 4—all bowled—in 1951-52; another all-bowled HT in 1957-58 and an HT in the grand final the same season; a bowled, bowled and lbw HT in 1962-63; 5 wickets in 6 balls (bowled, bowled, dot ball, bowled, lbw and bowled) in 1965-66; and the lucky seventh in 1974-75.

For his 1974-75 HT, he writes: 'We needed four wickets in my last over and I got 4 in 5 balls, and won'.

Apart from these seven HTs, Don deserved five more. For Melbourne Cricket Club v. Cricket Club of London on the Melbourne Cricket Ground (MCG) in 1974-75, Don had taken 2 in 2 when captain George Thoms (who had played one Test for Australia against West Indies in 1951-52) ran up and whispered to Don: 'The next man is Frank Russell, their President, and he has to get runs.' So Don bowled a donkey drop, Russell (who had vision in only one eye) swung wildly but missed and was bowled. A HT on the MCG—of all places—joy unconfined, but he remembered his captain's request and yelled: 'No ball!' The shocked English umpire commented: 'Oh dear, we do have a secret'.

Don again played on the MCG in March 1994 for the 29ers and bagged another 'moral' HT. Off the last ball of his first over, he had Michael York caught and with the first ball of his next over he bowled Peter Ashton. The next delivery hit the batsman ankle high in front of the middle stump and he yelled: 'Hat-trick on MCG!' But umpire Ian Stuart, with first-class experience, mumbled 'Not out'.

'Why?' Don asked.

'Oh no, I cannot give him out first ball', replied Stuart.

Don got his man in the same over leg-before and told Stuart: 'The batsman was more plumb first time than now', and Stuart agreed. The moral code of the Stuarts robbed him of his second HT on MCG, just as the code of Thoms & Moyes had robbed him of the first.

In 1956-57, Don captured 13 wickets for two runs for Victoria v. South Australia in the Australian Churches Union Carnival at Brisbane. He took 3 for 1 in the first innings and 10 for 1 in the second. He was three times on an HT in the second knock without converting it even once.

A remarkable character, Don Moyes.

SULTAN OF JUNIOR HTS

Not far behind Don Moyes for his HT appetite is Bob Newman of Batemans Bay, NSW. For Junior cricket (from Under-10 to Under-16), he performed six HTs—each in the A division. In 1962-63, he performed three HTs, two in one innings, for Miranda Magpies v. Boy's Town (Engadine) when he was 12.

Six years later when representing Sutherland Shires in Sydney, he achieved four HTs in the 1968-69 season.

Now Assistant Principal of Brooke Avenue Public School, Bob has made a comeback with the Entrance District CC in the Gosford-Wyong Competition where he captains the second-grade team. 'A couple of HTs would be very handy come semi-final time,' muses Bob, trying to recapture his 1960s magic.

GLOUCESTER'S PROUD MUM

For Matthews XI v. Waugh XI in Gloucester (NSW) Junior Cricket, eight-year-old Maryann Germon took an HT on her first day of playing cricket. More remarkable, it was in her very first over. Her mum Marie even remembers the exact date: 11 October 1986. 'Till now Maryann is the only female to take a hat-trick in Competition cricket in Gloucester District', she adds. The only sad part about the pioneering HT is that Maryann's third victim was her own brother. 'I guess that's one [incident] we will never live down in this house,' writes Marie.

Maryann has gone to bigger and better things. She organised a girl's primary school cricket team and won the NSW final in 1989. She has continued at Combined High School (CHS) level which won the State final of women's cricket twice. She was also selected to tour England and Ireland in June 1995 for four weeks with CHS NSW team.

Details of the HT scored by Bronwyn Clark, aged 13, are presented in the letter opposite. It seems hat-tricks run in the family; Bronwyn's 18 year old spin-bowling sister scored a top hat trick as well as running out an opposing player in one memorable club match.

WICKET WOMEN

Erica Sainsbury, statistician extraordinary of women's cricket, gives us the following information:

Hat-Tricks in Women's Tests: Only one; by Australia's outstanding cricketer Betty Wilson in the second Test against England at the St

To whom it may concern,

I was reading the January eddition of the Inside Edge. and I saw your letter on writting a book about Hat-Tricks that have happened to the readers It caught my attention right away

I am a 13 year old girl who lives in a country area called Dalwood 9km out of a small town Branxton. In my Primary School years I went to Branxton Public I'm now in Yr 8 One Friday afternoon in year 6 for sport we were playing cricket (obviously) and I was bowling 1st for my team. My 1st ball was a long way wide. I got alot of ribbing about that My next ball was straight on line. Our umpire (a teacher) suggested that I had the makings of a Denis Lillie- but I quickly said no a Simon O'Donnell my 3rd ball went dead straight and hit the other teams no.1 batsmans middle stump No 4 ball went much the same and knocked over the other opener. Ball no 5 a beautiful outswinger that nicked the outside edge of the number 3's bat and was beautifully caught by our diving keeper. That was my best cricket experience ever.

I hope that this will be alot of help 4 you.

From

P.S. DAMIEN Bronwyn Clark P.P.S.
MARTYN, JUSTIN
LANGER AND MATT Bronwyn Clark
HAYDEN ARE the
biggest LEGENDS

UP THE W.A. Warriors

Kilda Ground, Melbourne, on 21 February 1958. Betty took wickets with the first three deliveries of her 10th over in the first innings. She finished with innings figures of 7 for 7 and match analysis of 29.3-18-16-11. England's first innings total of 35 is the lowest recorded in Tests. Betty scored a century (a round 100) to become the *first* cricketer—male or female—to complete the double of 100 runs and 10 wickets (including an HT) in the same Test.

HTs in Limited-Over International: Only two such HTs, both coincidentally in the same week during the Fifth World Cup in England in 1993.

Off-spinner Carole Hodges (later Cornthwaite) of England took wickets with the third, fourth and fifth balls of her fifth over against Denmark on 20 July 1993, at Banstead Cricket Club, Surrey. All three of her victims were caught. This was Denmark's debut appearance in World Cup cricket and Carole's spell ended their innings.

New Zealand's medium-pacer Julie Harris captured wickets with the fifth and sixth balls of her seventh over and the first ball of her eighth against the West Indies on 26 July 1993, at Chiswick. Remarkably, all three wickets were lbw and the spell finished the Windies' resistance.

HTs in First-Class Cricket: Records are incomplete but the following have been recorded by Aussie women.

Spinner Muriel Picton took an HT in her only over (3 for 0) for the touring Australians against West of England on 27 May 1963, at Somerset. All three of her victims were caught, the score-book entry being 0WWW00.

Medium-pacer Karen Price (later Hill) took wickets with the last two balls of her sixth over and first ball of her seventh, to finish with 5 for 10 in 10 overs. This was for Australia v. East Midlands at Coalville on 7 July 1976.

Left-arm spinner Alisa Rowell took an HT in her 10th over for Queensland v. Tasmania in the Australian Championships in Adelaide on 10 January 1986. The first two wickets were caught by Michele Arnold, who later in the same tournament created an Australian first-class record by taking 9 for 29. Alisa's third victim was stumped and finished with 6 for 13; all six wickets were taken in her last 20 balls.

DRUNK YANK

HTs can be exhilarating, awe-inspiring, or spell-binding. But once it was intoxicating.

In an Annual Education Department match between NSW and Victoria at Centennial Park, Sydney, in 1980, Allan West performed what was, for want of a better word, a tipsy HT. Batting first, NSW made 204 off 40 overs. The visiting Victorians, who were well-wined and dined the night before were also supplied with beer-on-tap during lunch. With five wickets down for not many runs, Allan West was brought in to the attack.

'In the second over, I sent down a leg-cutter which the batsman chased and got a snick to the wicket-keeper. One off one. The next batsman was a victim of pre-match frivolities. Through bloodshot eyes he asked the umpire where the middle stump was and then placed his bat three inches outside the off-stump! I aimed straight for the stumps and the off-bail went flying. Two off two.

'To be honest, it was a soft second wicket. It was even more of a joke when the next man walked in—bat in one hand and a can of Fosters in the other. On somehow arriving near the stumps, he yelled in a broad American accent: "Howdy, y'all."

'What more could I ask for a hat-trick—a drunk Yank! I gently aimed at the stumps. The mini "septic tank" took a huge swing, missed and lost his middle stump. And I pulled off one of the easiest and most insignificant hat-tricks on record.'

Victorian Education Department, please note.

FROM THE AGONY END

When the captain says you are batting at no. 5, you don't worry about padding up at the start. Yet, no. 5 batsman José Coulson had to 'dress like a fireman' to face the fourth ball of the day. Batsmen nos 1, 3 and 4 got golden ducks and the bowler already had taken an HT with the first three balls. Oddly, the bowler was more nervous than José and the next four balls were wide. There were four golden ducks and two ducks in the innings as Rugby School team in England were shot out for 67 in 1994 and lost to Bedford Modern by five wickets.

HOLY HAT-TRICKS

Bob Chalmers, historian of Essendon and Broadmeadows Churches

Cricket Association (EBCCA), Victoria for over 20 years, gives the following nuggets on junior and 'paddock' cricket:

• Ian McTaggart took an HT with the first three balls of his opening over for Broughton-Miller B grade team against a shell-shocked St Johns Presbyterians side in 1935-36.

• Playing for St John's Presbyterians against Christ Church A grade side, Bruce Collings clean-bowled three batsmen with the last three balls in the first over of the match.

• In the Sunday School (Under-16) match in 1966-67, two young bowlers took all 10 wickets in an innings for their respective sides on the same afternoon. For Aberfeldie Baptists, Leigh Thornton took 10 for 8 (including an HT) against Pascoe Vale West Methodists, while Peter Kivisalu of St John's Presbyterians also bagged 10 for 8 (including five in his last five balls) v. Glenroy Presbyterians.

• Bruce Thornton, for St John's Presbyterians against North Essendon Church of Christ in 1967-68, was brought on to bowl with the score at 3 for 9. At the end of the over the score was 9 for 9. He had given marching orders to batsmen with ball nos 2, 3, 5, 6, 7 and 8. Thus he had taken 6 for 0—including 4 in 4.

• I. McPherson captured seven wickets for two runs for Christ Church Under-16 against Knox Presbyterians in 1946-47, claiming an HT in each of his first two overs.

• The feat of taking five wickets in five balls has been performed twice in Open Age matches in EBCCA cricket. They are by C. Groves for Kensington Methodists v. Moonie Ponds Methodists in a B grade match in 1912-13 and Jack Hosking v. Holy Trinity B in 1944-45.

• Bill Reilly (Pascoe Vale C v. St John's Presbyterians, 1963-64), scored 118 and took 4 for 16 including an HT. Earlier, in 1958-59, George Cranwell captaining Strathmore B v. Essenden Church of Christ scored 141 and captured 8 for 99 which included an HT.

• Bert Horsburg, the bowler, and Lindsay Hood, the keeper, combined brilliantly to stamp out three batsmen from North Essendon Presbyterians in 1930. The mode of dismissals for all three departing batsmen read: st. Hood b. Horsburg.

• Three HTs were recorded in the *same* match between Ascot Vale Congregationals and North Essendon in 1957-58. D. Robb took 12 for 24 (including an HT in both innings) for the former and M. Ross performed an HT in securing 7 for 54.

IT'S ALL HAPPENING

In a 40-overs B grade match on 15 October 1994, Tullangatta (Victoria) batted first and scored 103. At the end of the 39th over, Bandiana were 7 for 101 when Tim Chessan, 14, came in to bowl the last suspenseful over. His first two balls were hit for singles and Bandiana team had already avoided defeat and needed just one run to win in four balls with three wickets in hand. His third ball was blocked but with the fourth and fifth balls Chessan dismissed two— caught by mid-off and by himself. The no. 11 walked in amid high tension with fielders all around him.

In deathly silence, the last ball of the match struck the dazed batsman on the pads. Tim appealed for lbw, the batsmen took off for a leg bye and the leg umpire turned down a run-out appeal. However, in this commotion, nobody watched the main umpire's raised finger to declare the batsman out lbw. The match ended in a thrilling tie and Tim got an HT to savour. As Bill Lawry would have said, 'It's all happening'.

FALL GOES BEFORE PRIDE

Andrew Petty, aged 11, was diffident when asked by his captain to open the bowling for Kangaroo Under-12s against Research at Diamond Creek in Victoria on 3 November 1990. His first over was a wicket maiden and the next three were maidens. His captain obviously wanted a breakthrough and told him that the next over would be his last unless he took a wicket right away.

This fired Andrew up. First ball, BANG, middle stump. Second ball whizzed past the batsman's shoulder and the third one hit his pad on the full. 'Howzat?' 'Not out,' said the ump. Fourth ball hit the off-stump. Next man in was a six footer and 'as fat as a tank' but Andrew bowled him neck and crop, saying 'You beauty'. Last man in was thin and shaking like a leaf but it was Andrew who slipped and fell which turned his intended thunderbolt into a slow lollipop. 'As I stumbled to the ground I looked at the wickets which were crumbling. I couldn't believe it! I think I shook about 50 pairs of hands after that hat-trick', Andrew recalls. His figures: 5 overs, 5 maidens, 0 runs, 6 wickets.

SMASHING HAT-TRICKS

Many readers have told me about their all-bowled HTs. Here are a few samples:

• Darren Goodger, an active umpire for seven seasons in NSW, witnessed only one HT 'live'. In an Independent School Association first XI match between St Pius X College, Chatswood, and Pittwater Grammar School at Oxford Falls in December, 1992, the former were shot out for 25 runs. Jonathan Davis, the opening bowler, claimed the HT—knocking the middle-stump out of the ground each time.

• For Lane Cove against N.S. Baptists in an Under-16 Northern Suburbs Competition in November 1958, Hartley Anderson (now of the Australian Old Collegians fame) took 5 for 12 including an HT at Artarmon Reserve. He uprooted the middle stump three times in three balls.

• In a fourth-grade match, Len Brennan of Wallsend District Club, Newcastle, took 6 for 28 which included an all-bowled HT in his ninth over.

• Medium-pacer Simon McCarthy took 3 for 0 in three balls for Asquith Under-13s at Glenorie Oval No. 1 in March 1982. All his victims were clean-bowled.

• Warren Bagust performed seven HTs including a 5 in 6, but the one he recalls with delight was way back in 1951-52 in the NSW Churches A grade competition. In that season, he was on an HT 13 times before he got one (4 in 4) in the last match of the season for Canterbury Methodists. 'What made this so memorable was not that it was a 4 in 4 feat but that all four were clean bowled with identical wrong 'uns which hit the top of middle and off. I finished with 9 for 42.'

• Joseph Brockley, 17, took all 10 wickets for two runs in 11 balls— including a *triple* HT—in the Inter Divisional Ships Shield at Purfleet, Essex, on 17 May 1924. All his victims were clean bowled.

DEADLY LOBS
Slow off-spinner Jack Convey took an unusual HT for his Youth Club in August 1949. His victims were out lbw, stumped and stumped by Stan Senator falling to Jack's towering lobs. I can understand the victims getting stumped to high lobs, but lbw?

THE MHS
MHS does not stand for something we use to flavour exotic food. Rather it is an abbreviation for the Merv Hughes Syndrome of achieving a delayed HT (after his Perth performance in December 1988).

• Slow bowler Mark Preston performed a 'retarded' HT which took three overs and a week to complete—and dismissing only *two* different batsmen. For Parks Combine v. Doncaster CC in the Box Hill Reporter District Association in Tasmania on 10 and 17 December 1977, Mark was given the bowl when Doncaster were 8 wickets down. Off the last ball of this over he had a batsman caught. His reward? He was taken off but eventually brought back. Off his first ball he bowled no. 11 bat and he had two wickets in two balls.

The next week he scored 66 (his first fifty) and hit his first six. In Doncaster's second innings he was brought on after a long wait. 'I knew I was on a hat-trick but nobody else did. As luck would have it the batsman facing him was one he had dismissed in the first innings and he had him caught at cover.

'I was jumping up and down claiming a hat-trick while everyone else wondered as to what I was on about. They believed me only after checking the scorebook. The inscription on my ball reads:

Mark Preston
2 for 2 and 1 for 10 including Hat-trick
v. Doncaster C of C; 10 and 17 Dec. 1977

• On the other hand, Beau Mantor (age 16) of Bunburg, Western Australia (in 1990) and Gareth Thompson of North Parramatta (in 1989) who performed such delayed HTs were blissfully unaware of it. Beau did not know about his achievement till the scorer congratulated him, while Gareth realised that he had performed a hat-trick an hour after the end of play—when doing his grocery shopping.

TOBY'S 8 IN 8

Ronald (Toby) Eipeo was an outstanding school cricketer in Griffith (NSW). Bowling for Yoogali School against Griffith Convent in 1938, he dismissed eight batsmen in an eight-ball over and over-confident Convent was bundled out for 3 measly runs.

According to Lew Adams, now 70 and who had played against him: 'Toby's action was identical to Ashley Mallett's, sort of windmill action. A tall, rangy lad, Toby would practice in his father's farm for hours, bowling at a single stump—hitting it two times out of three. I believe the Eipeo Cup [in his honour] is still being played in that area.'

CHIRKY DOUBLE ACT

Steve Davies, aged 21, and Mike Williams, aged 30, grabbed HTs in consecutive overs for Chirk v. Ruthin Seconds at Holyhead Oval, Chirk (UK) in North Wales Cricket League on 6 August 1994. Chirk declared at 6 for 201 (Steve 30 not out, Mike 22 not out) and dismissed Ruthin for 50 (Steve 7-4-5-4, Mike 8-4-25-4).

Steve's HT victims were taken in the first three balls of his over and Mike's in the last three balls of his over as Ruthin collapsed from 1 for 28 to 8 for 28.

Steve and Mike work in a local electrical company, Steve as a cable jointer and Mike as a computer programmer. 'I was astonished,' Mike said after the HTs. 'For me to go and get the HT straight after Steve was just incredible.'

YOU WOULDN'T BELIEVE IT

Randwick wrist-spinner Tom Wood performed a rare HT against North Sydney at Coogee Oval in Sydney on 2 January 1977. All three of his victims were adjudged lbw. Wood bowled the final, spell-binding over with Norths needing 16 to win with five wickets intact and won the game for his team. To quote umpire Bruce Livingston (who deserves a bravery award): 'Ro Shelton hit widely across the line of flight and was plumb lbw. The next two batsmen, Dave Redgie and Steve Taylor, did exactly the same thing and each was dead in front. You wouldn't believe it.'

Livingston is no stranger to HTs. He performed two himself when posted in New Guinea by the Commonwealth Bank. He also took 5 for 85 against Queensland in his one Sheffield Shield appearance for NSW.

HAWKESBURY'S HISTORIC HT

Hawkesbury's opening bowler Paul Sullivan took the pioneering HT in his club's first- grade history against Sydney University in November 1994. In his first over after lunch on the second day, he bowled Gary Lennon, trapped Brendan Hill lbw and had Angus Sharp caught by wicket-keeper Matt Lang off successive deliveries.

Steve Davies (left) and Mike Williams grabbed hat-tricks in consecutive overs for Chirk XI in North Wales League on 6 August 1994. (Steve Davies)

FAMILY HAT-TRICKS

• On 14 January 1995, the Castle Hill Church of Christ team played Holy Trinity, Baulkham Hills at Kellyville in the NSW Churches C grade competition. Daniel Tomkins of Holy Trinity dismissed in three balls Geoff Hall, 42, his son David, 18, and his father Arthur, 67 (that's ages not runs); a rare HT to get three generations of one family. 'The family that plays together, gets out together,' concludes George Richards in Column 8 of the *Sydney Morning Herald*.

• Mark Page of Sholing Rambler's Cricket Club dismissed three Trant brothers, Tim, Simon and Patrick, in three balls—all three bowled by balls which hit the off-stump.

• Tony Matchett took three HTs—two at junior level and one at senior. He fondly—and guiltily—remembers the first one. He was then 10 and playing for Beverly Hills Cricket Club in the St George Under-12 competition in 1965. After dismissing 2 in 2, the next boy in was Marty Treasure, an exceptionally promising cricketer. Tony bowled an off-break, Marty danced down the pitch, missed and was hit on the pad. 'In hindsight, I should not have appealed, but I did. There is no way he was out,' he recalled. And the umpire, who was Tony's father, said, 'Out, son'. Marty looked incredulous. 'He had lost his wicket to a father and son combination,' Tony remembers after 30 years, still embarrassed.

• Norm Walsh, the captain of Essendon Baptist C grade team, took an HT with a difference against St Aidans in 1964-65. All three batsmen fell to catches behind the stumps by Norm's 57 year-old father, Norm Snr.

• Foxon brothers combined for a remarkable HT when playing for Hinckley Cricket Club Under-15s in 1979. The first batsman was caught by 13-year-old Richard off his brother Peter's bowling. Next ball, Stephen Foxon, 10, stumped the new batsman and Peter completed the HT by clean-bowling the next batsman. The square-leg umpire during this HT was their father.

• For Wakatu third grade v. Athletic Old Boys at Victory Square, New Zealand, on 30 January 1987, Alan Roberts ran out a batsman with a quick throw to his younger brother John at the bowler's end.

Next ball, John had the new batsman caught which completed the over. The bowler at the other end was Alan's elder brother Neil who bowled a batsman first ball. Although technically not a hat-trick, three brothers had combined uniquely to dismiss three batsmen in three balls.

Earlier in 1980-81, Alan had performed a hat-trick in a grade match; his third victim was caught by Neil at second slip.

• What a way to start and end a season! David Stenning, aged 12, started off the 1980 season by taking an HT for Melbourne Lodge School, Surrey v. Wallop School off his *first* three balls of the season in April. Batsmen nos 1, 3 and 4 were bowled for ducks. His brother, left-arm orthodox spinner Paul, aged 16, ended the season for Esher Cricket Club in September by taking an HT (caught, bowled, caught) in dark, gloomy conditions to win an evening club match.

• Matthew Selby, aged 11 and brother Hugh, aged 13, of St Ives, Sydney, performed HTs for different teams in December 1994. Matthew, normally an off-spinner, opened the bowling for St Ives North School v. Lindfield East. He bowled two batsmen and had one caught behind as father Rob, the Under-12 Coach, watched in admiration.

Hugh, selected in Gee Shield as a batsman, achieved an all-bowled HT two weeks later for St Ives v. Wahroonga in an Under-14 Hornsby-Ku-Ring-Gai competition match.

• The Mundin family had two HTs to celebrate on 16 May 1987. After 24 years of club cricket for South Lakeland club Ibis in Kendal (UK) without performing an HT, Brian took two in successive league matches, on 25 April and 16 May 1987. The first was for Kendal v. Conistron in Fourth Division when he took 5 for 25 and the second one was for Ibis A v. Galgate A. His second HT coincided with son Phillip's first on the *same* day. For Kirkbie Kendal v. neighbouring Dallam in an Under-15 match, Phillip claimed 5 for 3.

BEG YOURS?

For West Pennant Hills B2 grade match in January 1995, opening bowler Darryl Daniel took four wickets in four balls—but after a bit of drama. When Darryl took his first 2 in 2, the batting team (which supplies umpires in this type of cricket) changed the umpire. Off Darryl's third ball, the batsman nicked and the wicket-keeper caught it. The new umpire put his finger up very, very slowly; after hesitating. One of the fielders, believing the decision had gone against him, told off the umpire belligerently, 'Are you deaf or something?' Only then did the fielders realise that the umpire was wearing a hearing aid in *both* ears. He was replaced immediately. Umpire no. 3 had no hesitation in giving the next man out first ball.

Thus Daniel's top HT was unique—three different umpires had participated in it!

HE TOOK 5 IN 5, BUT WAS IT AN HT?

Barry Eastment, from Gordon, Sydney, has taken about 3000 wickets in all grades, including over 400 in first grade. Originally a fast-medium bowler, now he bowls slow off-spin without any run-up. He played for NSW Colts v. Queensland Colts in 1951 and was selected to represent USA v. Canada when studying at Howard University in 1957.

In a social match in February 1970, he dismissed five batsmen in as many balls but was it a hat-trick? This is how it happened. The

Brian Mundin (right) and son Phillip took hat-tricks on the same day, 16 May 1987, in Kendal, UK. *(Brian Mundin)*

rule for this match was that you cannot dismiss a batsman first ball. Bowling his gentle off-spin for Killara Tennis Club v. Roseville Tennis Club at Killara Oval in Sydney, Barry captured his first wicket, then bowled the next man first ball but he survived as per the 'rules'. Barry bowled him next ball. The third batsman was caught in the covers first ball but ruled not out. He was bowled next ball. The scorebook entry was puzzling: W Ⓦ W Ⓦ W — Ⓦ meaning out but still in!

Radio and TV personality David Lord wrote in his column next week that he could not decide whether the sequence constituted a super-top hat-trick, a hat-trick or wasn't a hat-trick at all.

On 20 March 1994, Barry, aged 62, did perform an HT in the Master's Cup for I. Zingari v. Lord Taverners at Acron Oval, St Ives, taking 5 for 0 in two overs. He feels he deserved 4 in 4 and figures of 6 for 0 but the square-leg umpire did not give the next batsman out stumped, although he was six inches out of the crease. 'That would have been a top hat-trick with a ball to come. Would history have repeated itself?' Barry wonders.

A ONE-MAN HAT-TRICK

Donald Noble Scott-Orr, the grand nephew of M. A. Noble, told me this strange story near M. A. Noble Stand during the topsy-turvy Sydney Ashes Test in January 1995. When batting for Kimcumber-Avoca against Ourimbah in a local first grade match in 1990 or 1991, he was caught by the wicket-keeper on the leg-side but umpire Stan Lansdowne said 'Not out'. Donald did not walk. Next ball, he was caught by the keeper on the off-side. A vociferous appeal this time was again ignored by the umpire. Donald did not walk. 'Why should I? Many times umpires give me wrongly out and I leave without a murmur'. Third ball, he was plumb lbw and Stan the man gave him out. Thus, Donald was, in a way, three HT victims rolled into one!

RIPLEY—WHERE ARE YOU?

• *The History of Radley College* relates this incredible story of W. E. W. Collins, 'a huge hitter and a ferocious bowler'. He claims to have dismissed three men in one delivery. 'The first victim was hit on the thumb and was led out bleeding profusely, his colleague fainted and the next man decided not to bat.'

• *Hill Chatter* of April 1974—a publication of the Sydney Branch of the Australian Cricket Society—tells another incredible tale (tall but true) under the heading 'Five Wickets Fell—But Only One Ball Was Bowled'. This is how it happened:

It was a two-day (Saturday afternoon) match in London. At the end of the first day, the batting side had lost five wickets. On the following Saturday one of the overnight not out batsmen caught the bus to Kennington instead of Kensington. He arrived late and was ruled out by the umpire. One wicket had thus fallen without a ball being bowled.

The first ball of the day was a no-ball which the batsman played to mid-on but was run out. Two wickets down—still no legitimate ball bowled. Next ball, a good one, was driven hard straight back and struck his batting partner on the head. The ball rebounded in the air and was caught. The chap with a cracked skull was carried off. Thus four men were out—and only one ball bowled.

The last man arrived at the crease but seeing there was no one to bat with, he was ruled out. Thus, the fifth wicket had 'fallen' while only one ball was bowled.

The story ends with the words: 'This I believe! I was there. One of the umpires.' It is signed 'Hoot', who we believe to be the late Mr Harold Gibson, whose collection was donated to the Australian Cricket Society in 1974.

NO KIDDING—6 IN 6, ALL BOWLED

Trevor Kidd, 12, clean bowled six batsmen in six balls for St. MartinSchool vs. Marian College in Johannesburg on 21 January 1992. He finished with 8 for 8 (all bowled).

TON 'N TRICK

Another South African, Johan van Niekerk, scored an unbeaten 102 and took all 10 wickets for 46-finishing the match with a hat trick. this was for Marlow Park v. Stoke Green in July 1995. 'They were a bit angry after the game,' he said. 'They thought I was too good to play against them.'

Appendix

(See also Postscript opposite Foreword)

HAT-TRICKS IN TEST CRICKET
(Figures accurate to 1 June 1995)
COUNTRY-WISE BREAK-UP

FOR	AGAINST									TOTAL
	Aus	Eng	SAf	WI	NZ	Ind	Pak	SL	Zim	
Aus	-	4	3	1	0	0	1	0	0	9
Eng	3	-	2	1	1	0	0	0	0	7
SAf	0	1	-	0	0	0	0	0	0	1
WI	2	0	0	-	0	0	1	0	0	3
NZ	0	0	0	0	-	0	1	0	0	1
Ind	0	0	0	0	0	-	0	0	0	0
Pak	0	0	0	0	0	0	-	0	0	0
SL	0	0	0	0	0	0	0	-	0	0
Zim	0	0	0	0	0	0	0	0	-	0
Total	5	5	5	2	1	0	3	0	0	21

TEST HAT-TRICKS

Bowler	Match	Venue	Season
F. R. Spofforth	Australia v. England	Melbourne	1878-79
W. Bates	England v. Australia	Melbourne	1882-83
J. Briggs	England v. Australia	Sydney	1891-92
G. A. Lohmann	England v. Sth Africa	Pt Elizabeth	1895-96
J. T. Hearne	England v. Australia	Leeds	1899
H. Trumble	Australia v. England	Melbourne	1901-02
H. Trumble	Australia v. England	Melbourne	1903-04

Bowler	Match	Venue	Season
T. J. Matthews[a]	} Australia v. Sth Africa	Manchester	1912
T. J. Matthews			
M. J. C. Allom[b]	England v. New Z'land	Christchurch	1929-30
T. W. J. Goddard	England v. Sth Africa	Johannesburg	1938-39
P. J. Loader	England v. West Indies	Leeds	1957
L. F. Kline	Australia v. Sth Africa	Cape Town	1957-58
W. W. Hall	West Indies v. Pakistan	Lahore	1958-59
G. M. Griffin	Sth Africa v. England	Lord's	1960
L. R. Gibbs	West Indies v. Australia	Adelaide	1960-61
P. J. Petherick[b]	New Zealand v. Pakistan	Lahore	1976-77
C. A. Walsh[c]	West Indies v. Australia	Brisbane	1988-89
M. G. Hughes[c]	Australia v. West Indies	Perth	1988-89
D. W. Fleming[b]	Australia v. Pakistan	Rawalpindi	1994-95
S. K. Warne	Australia v. England	Melbourne	1994-95

a T. J. Matthew took the hat-trick in each innings of the same match
b On Test debut
c Not all in the same innings

Note: In this group, Gibbs has taken most Test wickets (309) and has taken 5 wkts/ings most times (18). Lohmann has best bowling average (10.75) and best bowling figures (9-28). Briggs is the only one to score a Test century and Hughes only one to top 1000 Test runs.

DETAILS ON TEST HAT-TRICKS
(For countries involved and the venue, see the table above)

Bowler	Victims—How They Fell	Date
F. R. Spofforth	V.P.F.A. Royle b.3; F.A. MacKinnon b.0; T.Emmett c.0	2/1/1879
W. Bates	P.S. McDonnell b.3; G. Giffen c.0; G.J. Bonnor c.0	20/1/1883
J. Briggs	W.F. Giffen b.3; S.T. Callaway c.0; J.M. Blackham lbw 0	2/2/1892
G. A. Lohmann	F.J. Cook b.0; J. Middleton b.0; J.T. Willoughby c.0	14/2/1896

Bowler	*Victims—How They Fell*	*Date*
J. T. Hearne	C. Hill b.0; S.E. Gregory c.0; M.A. Noble c.0	30/6/1899
H. Trumble	A.O. Jones c.6; J.R. Gunn c.2; S.F. Barnes c.0	4/1/1902
H. Trumble	B.J.T. Bosanquet c.4; P.F. Warner c.11; A.F.A. Lilley lbw 0	8/3/1904
T. J. Matthews	R. Beaumont b.31; S.J. Pegler lbw 0; T.A. Ward lbw 0	28/5/1912
T. J. Matthews	H.W. Taylor b.21; R.O. Schwarz c.0; T.A. Ward c.0	28/5/1912
M. J. C. Allom	T.C. Lowry lbw 0; K.C. James c.0; F.T. Badcock b.0	10/1/1930
T. W. J. Goddard	A.D. Nourse c.73; N. Gordon st.0; W.W. Wades b.0	26/12/1938
P. J. Loader	J.D.C. Goddard b.1; S. Ramadhin c.0; R. Gilchrist b.0	25/7/1957
L. F. Kline	E.R.H. Fuller c.0; H.J. Tayfield lbw 0; N.A.T. Adcock c.0	3/1/1958
W. W. Hall	Mushtaq Md. lbw 14; Fazal Md. c.0; Nasim-ul-Ghani b.0	29/3/1959
G. M. Griffin	M.J.K. Smith c.99; P.M.Walker b.52; F.S. Trueman b.0	23/1/1960
L. R. Gibbs	K.D. Mackay lbw 29; A.T.W. Grout c.0; F.M. Misson b.0	30/1/1961
P. J. Petherick	Javed Miandad c.163; Wasim Raja c.0; Intikhab Alam c.0	10/10/1976
C. A. Walsh	A.J.C. Dodemaide c.22; M.R.J.Veletta c.10; G.M. Wood lbw 0	18&20/11/1988
M. G. Hughes	C.E.L. Ambrose c.8; B.P. Patterson c.1; C.G. Greenidge lbw 0	3&4/12/1988
D. W. Fleming	Aamer Malik c.65; Inzamam-ul-Haq lbw 0; Salim Malik c.237	9/10/1994
S. K. Warne	P.A.J. DeFreitas lbw 14; D. Gough c.0; D.E. Malcolm c.0	29/12/1994

NOTE: All no. 3 hat-trick victims made ducks, except Salim Malik who scored 237

109

FOUR WICKETS IN FIVE BALLS

Bowler	Match	Venue	Season
M. J. C. Alom *In his first Test—in his* *8th over* (W0WWW)	Eng v. N.Z.	Christchurch	1929-30
C.M. Old *In the same over* (WW0WW), *his 3rd ball was a no ball*	Eng v. Pak	Birmingham	1978
Wasim Akram *In the same over* (WW1WW), *a catch was dropped from the 3rd ball*	Pak v. W.I.	Lahore	1990-91

THREE WICKETS IN FOUR BALLS

Bowler	Match	Venue	Season
F. R. Spofforth	Australia v. England	The Oval	1882
F. R. Spofforth	Australia v. England	Sydney	1884-85
J. Briggs	England v. South Africa	Cape Town	1888-89
W. P. Howell	Australia v. South Africa	Cape Town	1902-03
E. P. Nupen	South Africa v. England	Johannesburg	1930-31
W. J. O'Reilly	Australia v. England	Manchester	1934
B. Mitchell	South Africa v. Australia	Johannesburg	1935-36
W. Voce	England v. Australia	Sydney	1936-37
R. R. Lindwall	Australia v. England	Adelaide	1946-47
K. Cranston[a]	England v. South Africa	Leeds	1947
C. N. McCarthy	South Africa v. England	Durban	1948-49
R. Appleyard	England v. New Zealand	Auckland	1954-55
R. Benaud	Australia v. West Indies	Georgetown	1954-55
Fazal Mahmood	Pakistan v. Australia	Karachi	1956-57
J. W. Martin	Australia v. West Indies	Melbourne	1960-61
L. R. Gibbs	West Indies v. Australia	Sydney	1960-61

Bowler	Match	Venue	Season
K. D. Mackay	Australia v. England	Birmingham	1961
W. W. Hall	West Indies v. India	Port-of-Spain	1961-62
D. Shackleton	England v. West Indies	Lord's	1963
G. D. McKenzie	Australia v. West Indies	Port-of-Spain	1964-65
F. J. Titmus[a]	England v. New Zealand	Leeds	1965
P. Lever	England v. Pakistan	Leeds	1971
D. K. Lillee	Australia v. England	Manchester	1972
D. K. Lillee	Australia v. England	The Oval	1972
C. M. Old[a]	England v. Pakistan	Birmingham	1978
S. T. Clarke	West Indies v. Pakistan	Karachi	1980-81
R. Hadlee	New Zealand v. Australia	Melbourne	1980-81
R. Shastri	India v. New Zealand	Wellington	1980-81
I. T. Botham	England v. Australia	Leeds	1985
Kapil Dev	India v. Australia	Adelaide	1985-86
C. G. Rackemann	Australia v. Pakistan	Adelaide	1989-90
D. E. Malcolm	England v. West Indies	Port-of-Spain	1989-90
Wasim Akram[a]	Pakistan v. West Indies	Lahore	1990-91
A. R. Border	Australia v. West Indies	Georgetown	1990-91
Wasim Akram	Pakistan v. England	Lord's	1992
S. K. Warne	Australia v. England	Brisbane	1994-95

[a] K. Cranston, F. J. Titmus, C. M. Old and Wasim Akram each took four wickets in an over.

HAT-TRICKS IN FIRST-CLASS CRICKET
FOUR WICKETS IN FOUR BALLS

Bowler	Match	Venue	Season
J. Wells	Kent v. Sussex	Brighton	1862
G. Ulyett	Lord Harris' XI v. NSW	Sydney	1878-79
G. Nash	Lancashire v. Somerset	Manchester	1882
J. B. Hide	Sussex v. MCC and Ground	Lord's	1890

Bowler	Match	Venue	Season
F. J. Shacklock	Nottinghamshire v. Somerset	Nottingham	1893
A. D. Downes	Otago v. Auckland	Dunedin	1893-94
F. Martin	MCC & Ground v. Derbyshire	Lord's	1895
A. W. Mold	Lancashire v. Nottinghamshire	Nottingham	1895
W. Brearley[a]	Lancashire v. Somerset	Manchester	1905
S. Haigh	MCC v. Army XI	Pretoria	1905-06
A. E. Trott[b]	Middlesex v. Somerset	Lord's	1907
F. A. Tarrant	Middlesex v. Gloucestershire	Bristol	1907
A. Drake	Yorkshire v. Derbyshire	Chesterfield	1914
S. G. Smith	Northamptonshire v. Warwickshire	Birmingham	1914
H. A. Peach	Surrey v. Sussex	The Oval	1924
A. F. Borland	Natal v. Griqualand West	Kimberley	1926-27
J. E. H. Hooker[a]	NSW v. Victoria	Sydney	1928-29
R. K. Tyldesley[a]	Lancashire v. Derbyshire	Derby	1929
R. J. Crisp	Western Province v. Griqualand West	Johannesburg	1931-32
R. J. Crisp	Western Province v. Natal	Durban	1933-34
A. R. Gover	Surrey v. Worcestershire	Worcester	1935
W. H. Copson	Derbyshire v. Warwickshire	Derby	1937
W. A. Henderson	N.E. Transvaal v. Orange Free State	Bloemfontein	1937-38
F. Ridgway	Kent v. Derbyshire	Folkestone	1951
A. K. Walker[c]	Nottinghamshire v. Leicestershire	Leicester	1956
S.N. Mohol	President's XI v. Combined XI	Poona	1965-66
P. I. Pocock	Surrey v. Sussex	Eastbourne	1972
S. S. Saini[a]	Delhi v. Himachal Pradesh	Delhi	1988-89
D. Dias	W. Province (Suburbs) v. Central Province	Colombo	1990-91

a Not all in the same innings
b Trott achieved another hat-trick in the same innings of this, his benefit match
c Walker dismissed Firth with the last ball of the first innings and Lester, Tompkin and Smithson with the first three balls of the second innings, a unique feat.

FIVE WICKETS IN SIX BALLS
(Including a hat-trick)

Bowler	Match	Venue	Season
W. H. Copson	Derbyshire v. Warwickshire	Derby	1937
W. A. Henderson	N.E. Transvaal v. Orange Free State	Bloemfontein	1937-38
P. I. Pollock	Surrey v. Sussex	Eastbourne	1972

TWO HAT-TRICKS IN SAME MATCH

Bowler	Match	Venue	Season
A. Shaw	Nottinghamshire v. Gloucestershire	Nottingham	1884
A. E. Trott[a]	Middlesex v. Somerset	Lord's	1907
T. J. Matthews	Australia v. South Africa	Manchester	1912
C. W. L. Parker	Gloucestershire v. Middlesex	Bristol	1924
R. O. Jenkins	Worcestershire v. Surrey	Worcester	1949
J. S. Rao[b]	Services v. Northern Punjab	Amritsar	1963-64
Amin Lakhani	Combined XI v. Indians	Multan	1978-79

a Trott performed a 4 in 4 and a hat-trick in the same innings
b Rao performed two hat-tricks in the same innings

MOST HAT-TRICKS
(Minimum 3)

SEVEN TIMES: D. V. P. Wright

SIX TIMES: T. W. J. Goddard, C. W. L. Parker

FIVE TIMES: S. Haigh, V. W. C. Jupp, A. E. G. Rhodes, F. A. Tarrant

FOUR TIMES: R. G. Barlow, J. T. Hearne, J. C. Laker, G. A. R. Lock, G. G. Macaulay, T. J. Matthews, M. J. Procter, T. Richardson, F. R. Spofforth, F. S. Trueman

THREE TIMES: W. M. Bradley, H. J. Butler, S. T. Clarke, W. H. Copson,
R. J. Crisp, J. W. H. T. Douglas, J. A. Flavell,
A. P. Freeman, G. Giffen, K. Higgs, A. Hill,
W. A. Humphreys, R. D. Jackman, R. O. Jenkins,
A. S. Kennedy, W. H. Lockwood, E. A. McDonald,
T. L. Pritchard, J. S. Rao, A. Shaw, J. B. Statham,
M. W. Tate, H. Trumble, D. Wilson, G. A. Wilson

HAT-TRICK ON DEBUT

Bowler	Match	Venue	Season
H. Hay	Sth Aust v. Lork Hawke's XI	Adelaide	1902-03
H. A. Sedgwick	Yorkshire v. Worcestershire	Hull	1906
V. B. Ranjane	Maharashtra v. Saurashtra	Poona	1956-57
J. S. Rao	Services v. Jammu & Kashmir	Delhi	1963-64
R. O. Estwick	Barbados v. Guyana	Bridgetown	1982-83
S. A. Ankola	Maharashtra v. Gujarat	Poona	1988-89
J. Srinath	Karnataka v. Hyderabad	Secunderabad	1989-90
S. P. Mukherjee	Bengal v. Hyderabad	Secunderabad	1989-90

Note: J. S. Rao performed two more hat-tricks in his next match

CENTURY AND HAT-TRICK IN SAME MATCH

Bowler	Match	Venue	Season
G. Giffen	Australians v Lancashire, (13 & 113; 6-55∴)	Manchester	1884
W. E. Roller	Surrey v Sussex, (204; 4-28∴ & 2-16) – unique	The Oval	1885
W. B. Burns	Worcestershire v Gloucestershire (102*; 3-56∴ & 2-21)	Worcester	1913
J. W. C. Jupp	Sussex v Essex (102*; 6-61∴ & 6-78)	Colchester	1921

Bowler	Match	Venue	Season
R. E. S. Wyatt	MCC v Ceylon (124; 5-39∴)	Colombo	1926-27
L. N. Constantine	West Indians v Northamp'shire (107; 7-45∴ & 6-67)	Northampton	1928
D. E. Davies	Glamorgan v Leicestershire (139; 4-27 & 3-31∴)	Leicester	1937
V. M. Merchant	Perreira XI v Sir Mehta XI (1 & 142; 3-31∴ & 0-17)	Bombay	1946-47
M. J. Procter	Gloucestershire v Essex (51 & 102; 3-43 & 5-30∴– all lbw)	Westcliff–on–Sea	1972
M. J. Procter	Gloucestershire v Leicestershire, (122; 0-32 & 7-26∴)	Bristol	1979

* = not out; ∴ = including a hat-trick

TWO FIFTIES AND HAT-TRICK IN SAME MATCH

Bowler	Match	Venue	Season
J. G. Lomax	Somerset v Notting'shire (80 & 53; 0-7 & 4-15∴)	Weston–Super–Mare	1958
M. J. Procter	Gloucestershire v Essex (51 & 102; 3-43 & 5-30∴—all lbw)	Westcliff-on-Sea	1972
R. A. Woolmer	MCC v Australians (55 & 85; 4-45∴ & 0-62)	Lord's	1975
Imran Khan	Sussex v Warwickshire (94 & 64; 0-8 & 6-6∴)	Birmingham	1983
Wasim Akram	Lancashire v Surrey (58 & 98; 5-58∴ & 3-58)	Southport	1988
C. J. van Heerden	Orange Free State v Natal (56 & 65*;1-55 & 3-14∴)	Bloenfontein	1990-91

* = not out; ∴ = including a hat-trick

(List perhaps not complete. This table courtesy of Andrew Samson, *The Cricket Statistician*, Vol. 75, Autumn 1991)

HAT-TRICKS IN SHEFFIELD SHIELD CRICKET

Bowler	Match	Venue	Season
W. W. Armstrong	Vic v. NSW	Melbourne	1902-03
A. J. Y. Hopkins	NSW v. SA	Sydney	1903-04
H. I. Ebeling	Vic v. Qld	Melbourne	1928-29
C. V. Grimmett	SA v. Qld	Brisbane	1928-29
J. E. H. Hooker[a]	NSW v. Vic	Sydney	1928-29
A. K. Walker	NSW v. Qld	Sydney	1948-49
J. Treanor	NSW v. Qld	Brisbane	1954-55
G. F. Rorke	NSW v. Qld	Sydney	1958-59
A. K. Davidson	NSW v. WA	Perth	1962-63
D. Robins	SA v. NSW	Adelaide	1965-66
R. F. Surti	Qld v. WA	Perth	1968-69
W. Prior	SA v. NSW	Adelaide	1975-76
L. S. Pascoe	NSW v. SA	Adelaide	1980-81
P. M. Clough	Tas v. NSW	Hobart	1982-83
J. R. Thomson	Qld v. WA	Brisbane	1984-85
D. R. Gilbert	NSW v. Vic	Sydney	1984-85

(a) Hooker is the only one to capture 4 wickets in 4 balls in Sheffield Shield.

Note: W. J. Holdsworth (NSW v. Tasmania, Hobart, 1991-92) was on a hat-trick *three* times, but the third batsman eluded him every time. Holdsworth subsequently took a hat-trick for the touring Australians against Derbyshire at Derby in 1993.

HAT-TRICKS IN LIMITED-OVERS INTERNATIONALS (LOI)

Bowler	Match	Venue	Season
Jalal-ud-Din	Pakistan v. Australia	Hyderabad (Pak.)	1982-83
B. A. Reid	Australia v. New Zealand	Sydney	1985-86
C. J. Sharma	India v. New Zealand	Nagpur	1987-88
Wasim Akram	Pakistan v. West Indies	Sharjah	1989-90
Wasim Akram	Pakistan v. Australia	Sharjah	1989-90

Bowler	Match	Venue	Season
Kapil Dev	India v. Sri Lanka	Calcutta	1990-91
Aaqib Javed	Pakistan v. India	Sharjah	1991-92
D. K. Morrison	New Zealand v. India	Napier	1993-94
Waqar Younis	Pakistan v. New Zealand	East London	1994-95

Note: Sharma is the only one to perform a hat-trick in a World Cup match. All of his victims were bowled.

Reid's hat-trick was achieved in two overs.

Wasim Akram is the only one to achieve an LOI hat-trick *twice* (in the same city).

DETAILS OF LOI HAT-TRICKS
(For countries involved and the venue, see table above)

Bowler	Victims—How They Fell	Date
Jalal-ud-Din	R. W. Marsh b.1; B. Yardley c.0; G. F. Lawson b.0	20 Sept. 1982
B. A. Reid	R. W. Blair c.3; E. B. McSweeney c.1; S. R. Gillespie b.0	29 Jan. 1986
C. J. Sharma	K. R. Rutherford b.36; I. D. S. Smith b.0; E. J. Chatfield b.0	31 Oct. 1987
Wasim Akram	P. J. L. Dujon b.6; M. D. Marshall b.0; C. E. L. Ambrose b.0	14 Oct. 1989
Wasim Akram	M. G. Hughes b.9; C. G. Rackermann b.0; T. M. Alderman b.0	4 May 1990
Kapil Dev	R. S. Mahanama c.5; S. T. Jayasuriya c.5; R. J. Ratnayake lbw 0	4 Jan. 1991
Aaqib Javed	R. J. Shastri lbw 15; M. D. Azharuddin lbw 0; S. R. Tendulkar lbw 0	25 Oct. 1991
D. K. Morrison	Kapil Dev b.17; S. A. Ankola b.0; N. R. Mongia b.0	25 Mar. 1994
Waqar Younis	C. Z. Harris b.18; C. Pringle b.0; R. P. de Groen b.0	19 Dec. 1994

Aaqib Javed's hat-trick was the classiest in LOIs, with world-class batsmen Shastri, Azharuddin and Tendulkar as his victims.

Index